BUSINESS VALUATION BLUEBOOK

How Successful Entrepreneurs Price, Buy, Sell and Trade Businesses

"Small business is America's engine of free enterprise. Ownership of a small business offers opportunity, profit, choice, and ultimately freedom. Understanding business valuation does more to help entrepreneurs realize these benefits when they buy, operate, and sell than anything else."

Chad Simmons

Facts On Demand Press

BUSINESS VALUATION BLUEBOOK

How Successful Entrepreneurs
Price, Buy, Sell and Trade Businesses

Edited by Gary D. Walker
Printed in the United States by Victor Graphics, Inc.

ISBN-10: 1-889150-55-X
ISBN-13: 978-1-889150-55-0
Copyright ©2008 by Chad Simmons

4200 Somerset, Suite 245
Prairie Village, KS 66208
Voice: 913-648-7747   Fax: 913-385-7747
Chad@ChadJSimmons.com

Facts on Demand Press
PO Box 27869
Tempe, AZ 85285-7869
Voice: 800-929-3811   Fax: 800-929-3810
Website: www.brbpub.com

Publisher's Cataloging-in-Publication

Simmons, Chad.
    Business valuation bluebook : how successful
entrepreneurs price, buy, sell and trade businesses /
Chad Simmons. -- 4th ed.
    p. cm.
    Includes index.
    ISBN-13: 9781889150550
    ISBN-10: 188915055X

    1. Business enterprises--Valuation--Handbooks,
manuals, etc. 2. Sale of business enterprises--
Handbooks, manuals, etc. 3. Business enterprises--
Purchasing--Handbooks, manuals, etc.   I. Title.

HG4028.V3S558 2009   658.1'6
                        QBI08-600348

About the Author

Chad Simmons is an expert on small business valuation. He teaches what he does and does what he teaches—a symbol of today's entrepreneur.

Chad gained national standing in his franchise company selling small businesses. He rose through the ranks to become the company's president and a principal stockholder. His company was America's largest country real estate franchiser. In addition to rural property sales, the company sold $40 to $50 million of small businesses and commercial properties each year. Afterward, he wrote the *Business Valuation Bluebook*, describing his small business valuation techniques.

Numerous colleges have acquired his materials for classroom use. Chad's books and seminars have been included in the prestigious CCIM continuing education program sponsored by the National Association of Realtors®. He has taught small business valuation, approved for continuing education credit in several states, for nearly twenty years nationwide.

His most recent venture is the launch of CEband, an Internet company that provides professional seminars online including Small Business Valuation. His Internet delivery system is certified by two prestigious organizations: the Association of Real Estate License Law Officials (ARELLO) and the International Distance Education Certification Center (IDECC). His Small Business Valuation online seminar has been used as continuing education credit for real estate, appraisal and insurance and related business professionals. This and other courses may be viewed at www.ceband.com. He is also an active real estate investor. Chad's hobbies include travel, amateur astronomy, woodworking, reading and spending time with his family in Leawood, Kansas. He enjoys visualizing and executing ideas to improve business results.

Other Books and Works by Chad Simmons
The Anonymous Entrepreneur
Small Business Valuation Online

Look Who's Talking About the
Business Valuation Bluebook

"It doesn't take a hardball negotiator to buy 'under the market' and profit from the first day of ownership," says Chad Simmons, president of CEband and author of the *Business Valuation Bluebook*, which can help with calculating the value of your target. "When the asking price is clearly too high, as is often the case, presenting a realistic value to a seller will cause them to reduce the price if they are motivated to sell—or terminate discussions if they are not," Simmons says. "Either way, you win."

- quote from article in the April/May
   issue of *MyBusiness*

MyBusiness, the small business magazine from NFIB, serves as one of the primary means of communication with 600,000 small business members of the National Federation of Independent Business, one of the nation's largest lobbying groups.

Table of Contents

SECTION I—TECHNIQUES

SECTION 2—STRATEGY & TACTICS

Introduction— Business Valuation

An Answer You Need Right Now

Business indicators of value help entrepreneurs cash out with a big profit when they sell a business. It is how wealthy entrepreneurs recognize and snap up business bargains before others notice. You don't have to study a 600-page book to learn how to value a business, and you don't need to spend $125 on a book you don't have time to read, especially when the business of your interest might exist on Main Street, not Wall Street. The *Business Valuation Bluebook* is the bottom line of business valuation—a solution that fits the problem.

Know the Nuts and Bolts of Value

The *Business Valuation Bluebook* shows you how to use techniques that help you work so fast and accurately, few can argue with your conclusions. You'll learn effective phrases that help you become a negotiating sledgehammer. Real-world tips will improve your earning power whether you are a business buyer, manager or seller. They all work and are fully explained, with examples, so you can use them right away. For those who want results, not research, start by reading the first appendix, "Shortcuts." It provides the quick start that may be desired.

Maximize Your Return

Overstating or underestimating business value by a small percent can cost thousands. Indicators of value in this book can help you avoid this costly mistake. Plus, they can help you make as much or more when you buy. For example, my first-use application of these techniques earned me $100,000! From a $1 investment, my first acquisition netted $50,000 cash profit in 18 months. Still another business venture, when sold, returned a powerful $167 for every dollar invested. You can learn to use these indicators of value and enjoy results like these.

Let's Be Clear

The *Business Valuation Bluebook* describes indicators of business value and how to calculate them. These are a useful, powerful solution that meets most of the needs of small business entrepreneurs, but they should not be confused with a formal "valuation" that is performed by a qualified business appraiser. They are not the same thing. However, for easier reading, the terms "indicators of value" and "value or valuation" are used interchangeably throughout the *Business Valuation Bluebook*.

Exercise Caution!

The material in this book is provided for information purposes only. In all cases, readers are advised to seek the advice of qualified business professionals including (but not limited to) those offering tax, legal, appraisal and accounting expertise. The author, publisher and related parties involved with the development or distribution of this book and related materials assume no responsibility or liability for the consequences, good or bad, of your use of this information.

A Word from the Author

In Hard Times, All the Rules Change: A Quick Crash Course for Buyers and Sellers

One of the most important things business sellers must consider in difficult times is how to attract the largest number of buyers to their offerings. Attracting interested buyers increases the chances a business will sell for the highest price, in the shortest time, and with the least amount of effort. And this is what every seller ultimately desires.

In times like these, there is a lot of uncertainty in the economy, and most of this comes from the financial sector. Banks have money, but are reluctant to make business loans because they have been so badly burned by the sub-prime crisis. Prospective borrowers of any kind are painted with the sub-prime brush and the accompanying eye of skepticism. Small business sellers must understand this, because when offering their businesses for sale, two other parties must be considered: a buyer and a financier/bank.

To their disappointment, buyers are quickly learning under-writing guidelines for a small business loan are rising—it's harder to qualify. And this translates to higher lending standards for an ac-quisition target—a business—too. These changes in lending guide-lines have the twin effect of creating more pressure on the business and buyer to perform and making financing more costly. That, in turn, can have a significant effect on business value. If these factors are not coordinated well in advance of a loan request, the financ-ing is not likely to occur and, therefore, neither will the sale of the business.

But there is hope, and history is the best teacher. These times are not so different from what we saw in the late 1970s and early 1980s when interest rates were 18 percent. Back then, the rapidly rising costs of financing were making deals that had been reasonable completely unqualified. Buyers were walking away. Sellers could not sell. The market was very depressed. But, there were solutions available that enabled many to sell despite these unfavorable economic conditions.

Seller Financing

The strategy many used to succeed in those times can be used again today. Recall, attracting a larger pool of buyers to an offering is the first step toward creating a sale. And that can be accomplished with seller financing. This is possible because a seller is often more compliant than a bank when it comes to financing his own business. And the package of financing he offers is likely to be less costly. These two factors come together to help sellers hold up the value of their business, which is a very important consideration for any seller. So, back from the archives of earlier lessons, we find that seller financing is a handy tool to use in times like these.

Benefits of Seller Financing

There are many benefits to be had from offering seller financing when selling or buying a business. Most important of these, however, is the impact it will have on the creation of a buyer's market. Recall that this is the most important goal. Look at it this way: If there are 10 buyers looking for a small business and there are two businesses available, but one is offered for cash and the other one is offered with seller financing, how many of those buyers will inquire about the last one first? The answer is all of them. This is because they immediately see that seller financing is a path of least resistance and lower cost. Plus, it implies a degree of security the cash offering does not. Buyers will think *If the seller is willing to finance his own business, then he must be pretty confident that it is a good business.*

So an offering to sell a business that appeals to the largest pool of available buyers is the key to selling a business. And an attractive value proposition is just the ticket to getting this accomplished. There are other techniques, too, that can lower or improve the value even more—sometimes dramatically. I want to share a personal story about what can be done when you combine these with seller financing to strengthen an offering and attract more buyers.

When I was an aspiring young business broker looking for a business listing, I came upon a nice little "mom and pop" hamburger/ice cream restaurant. It was very clean and looked like it was doing a good, steady business. So I bought lunch and observed the place until I figured out who the owner might be so I could introduce myself. He was an older gentleman who ran the front and cashier window while his wife did all the cooking in back. After catching his attention, I asked if he would ever consider selling his business.

He said, "Sure, for $150,000 cash on the barrel-head" very affirmatively. Next, I asked if he had ever listed it with a broker, and he turned very negative.

"I listed our place with a broker a year ago," he spouted, "and they never showed our property to a single buyer. So I don't want anything to do with brokers."

It is always best to be very upfront in real estate transactions, so I told him I was a broker but would not attempt to list his property. I asked how much help the other broker gave him in pricing the property and structuring the offer so it would attract the most buyers. He said, "None." Next, I asked if there had ever been any time or attention given to justifying the price. Again, he said, "No." This is when I said, "Well, that could be your problem, and if you want, I would be happy to study this for you and give you my thoughts. If you like what you hear, you can list the property. If not, it's been a nice place to have lunch." He said, "Fair enough."

Prepare the Books

The first thing I did was ask him for five years of financial statements describing his business income, expenses, and net profit. After a few days, he delivered these to me, but they were his handwritten notes. No good. I asked for the financials from his accountant and he obliged quickly. Then I went to work.

After concluding my review, I returned to his business when there were no customers around so I could share my thoughts with him in privacy. I said, "After studying your business, I've determined what the problem really is—you are not attracting enough buyers. Look, you want $150,000 cash for the business and the real estate. But there are not a lot of buyers for a smaller business of this size with that kind of money. You really need to sell your business for $27,500." At this point his eyes got wide and he yelled, "Ma, come out here and listen to what this young man just said to me!"

I thought I was about to become a murder statistic but quickly continued by saying, "And you need to take a 50 percent down payment and finance the other half for three years at 10 percent interest."

The seller was dumbstruck, but before he could come after me with a meat cleaver, I quickly said, "But you are keeping your real estate and will turn it into rental property. You will get a rent payment every month in addition to your monthly payment on the business. Most importantly, how many more people do you think can afford to buy a business for $27,500 than can afford to buy one for $150,000?"

He said, "Well, a lot more." This is when I said, "Right, and that's the name of the game. Make your business appealing to as many buyers as possible because these are tough times and I'm trying to help you do one thing: sell your business. And to do so, it will take buyers, as many as we can get."

Believe it or not, they both agreed and listed their business with me. I didn't even have to ask for the listing contract—they offered. I sold their business in 41 days! And the sellers enjoyed the benefits of rental property to support their fixed income needs.

This is an example of shifting strategies to accommodate tough times, and an example of how effective it can be. In this example there were actually two strategies at work. Seller financing was the first, but separating out the real estate was the second because it created a major price reduction. This is important because business buyers seldom want or need to buy a parcel of investment real estate they often cannot afford. Their goal is to buy a source of cash flow that is large enough to support their family from their applied labor and profits. So sellers often err when including real estate with a business they are attempting to sell. The price becomes too high and disqualifies many good buyers. Just sell the buyer the business and after a year or so, when there is a good track record of making rent payments, the real estate can be sold to the business owner or another buyer as a real estate investment.

Remember: Hard times call for smart actions. If you want to sell a business in times like these, the tools described above are just two of the things you can do to get results. But there are more!

In Times Like These

As I write this, the price for a barrel of oil has risen to nearly $150 and fallen back to about $60. This has created havoc in the United States economy. The S&P 500 Stock Index has declined nearly 40 percent in the past 12 months and daily swings in value are of historic proportions. Unemployment is rising to levels not seen in two decades. The problem is this: Something that looks like a good deal today might not look so appealing 90 days or six months from now. So how is one to know if anything is really a good deal at all? The secret is to understand the indicators of value that are intrinsic to a business. This makes it possible to estimate value during normal times and calculate the discount, if any, available in times like these. And that is what business valuation is all about.

It also follows that tough times are good times for buyers interested in small business ownership. The supply and demand relationship of small businesses for sale is out-of-balance, so they have more to choose from and can negotiate a better value for what they choose. Sellers with the professional objectivity to correctly assess the field of opportunities available to business buyers in times like these will adjust accordingly, or, they will not sell anything.

So here are some rules of the road to keep in mind if you are a buyer or a seller. Pricing with a view to these will help flatten the landscape of opportunity so both can navigate towards successful acquisition.

Make Money When You Buy

The best time to make money in a business is when you buy it. And the most money can be made, through negotiation, with the least amount of effort. Buying under the market creates a cushion of value buyers need to prevent losses that can easily occur during the first year or two of ownership. That's so important because if, for some reason, a buyer needs to make a quick exit and sell, buying "right" makes this possible because one can pass on an attractive offering to someone else and minimize any financial loss. In times like these, where buyers are in limited supply, making money when you buy is a very real possibility. And the key is knowing business value and building the case that supports it.

Businesses Are Often Overpriced

Remember, sellers often price their business for sale based on the amount of debt they have and/or some amount of capital gain set arbitrarily. The logic supporting this value fails quickly when put to the test of financial justification as described by the valuation techniques outlined in this book. It becomes an opportunity to "recalculate" the value and negotiate with superior logic.

Offers Are Often Unrealistic

Buyers often make the same mistake as sellers and "fire off" unrealistically low offers that are not supported by good logic. This serves only to alienate a seller, and what might have been a workable transaction ends before it has a chance to begin.

Build a Case for Value

The key to effectively negotiating a purchase price involves two ingredients: highly motivated parties to the transaction and a compelling value that is well supported by valuation methods used in this book. Get permission to perform a value analysis and know the business value early using the premise that it is an attempt to confirm the seller's asking price— which it is. Once this is completed, it is a small step to calculate what the business really IS worth. And if, in the opinion of the buyer, that is within reason and likely to be considered by a seller, it becomes the beginning of negotiations.

Most Sellers Are in the Dark
When It Comes to Establishing Value

Many sellers of a successful business are very good at running their operation. Few, however, have any idea of what the business is worth or how to determine its value. This requires a different set of skills from running the business and more professional objectivity than they may possess. It is a smart buyer's opportunity to take the lead in negotiations, moving them in their favor.

The Best Logic Usually Wins

When buying a business, money talks—not the money a buyer has to pay, but the money a business can create, or its cash flow. The procedure of extrapolating that directly and by multiple means into a value range and offering price is straightforward and logical. In situations where sellers will not listen to reason, it is better to move on, remembering that the deal of a lifetime comes along every forty-five days in times like these.

Buy Smart!
There Are Many Choices...

It's difficult to know what type of business to buy. The answer depends mostly on the investor's personality. That said, it is still wise to recognize some businesses do perform better during times of economic uncertainty. In times like these where stability is desirable, the best businesses to buy often include some of the following types:

HOME DELIVERY: More and more people are operating out of their homes using the Internet to buy products and services. The price of fuel has an impact on delivery companies. But the loss of convenience and fuel costs borne by customers (when home delivery is not present) can be even greater. This simply means companies that offer some form of home delivery are positioned to do better than those that don't.

CLOSE TO HOME FUN: For many, extended vacations at distant locations may give way to resorts and entertainment venues that are closer to home. This could be especially true among vacation spots that have been in business for a few decades. Nostalgia sells and what is old can easily become new again with a little marketing.

ENVIRONMENTALLY SENSITIVE: Going Green is a smart thing to do. It is a major societal trend in the United States and even globally. Businesses that offer environmentally responsible products and services fill the customers' need to "feel" they are indirectly supporting a cleaner environment. It also helps avoid the impression they are damaging the environment by not buying Green. Very importantly, going Green is one of those standards that may not make any money where present but could avoid losing revenue when it is not.

HEALTH & NATURAL CARE: We Americans want to feel good and look good. But, we are getting older and don't like it very much. Products and services that promise to help keep us feeling younger, looking younger, and feeling healthier will enjoy growing popularity. And here is an industry with the double-down marketing potential. As consumers discover their new, youthful self contradicting their chronological age, the demand will increase as they continue to age. The future for natural care products and services should be bright.

DO-IT-YOURSELF SOLUTIONS: In times like these, people are forced to turn to themselves to get things done. This is because it costs money to hire others, and many are cutting budgets. Also, there may be fewer business service providers available due to these difficult times. So, businesses offering these types of products and solutions capitalize on consumers' desire for greater independence and autonomy indicated in times like these.

THE BIG THREE: FOOD, FUEL AND LIQUOR: Simply put, people need and want to eat, heat, drive and drink (but not necessarily simultaneously). They always have and always will want these things. And, curiously, the amount of food, fuel and liquor does not change too significantly with good or bad economic times. So businesses offering these products do not experience the extreme volatility that unfavorably affects the revenue of many other companies. That makes them good businesses to own.

Ensure a Good Fit

The first question successful entrepreneurs ask themselves when considering a business acquisition is *How do I want to spend my time?* This is a very important question with a revealing answer. Business ownership is not a "hands-off" affair and will require a commitment of time and energy. It is best to know what will be involved before taking this very costly leap. A good way to choose a business that's a good fit for you is to consider the following:

BUY WHAT YOU KNOW: This is a powerful way to remove much of the risk associated with buying a business. Any acquisition involves some type of learning curve, which is a time of great risk. Where the entrepreneur's product/service knowledge is present, it's easier to learn how the business is run. But learning that in addition to all that must be known about the merchandise or services sold is a more daunting proposition and one to consider very carefully. There is likely to be less risk when buying what is familiar.

BUY WHAT YOU LIKE: Business ownership will be next to impossible if the entrepreneurs do not enjoy working for themselves in a profession of their choosing. This involves a different level of accountability than any job. On many occasions, a new business owner must handle unique situations and hasn't the foggiest idea of what to do. Worse, there is no one to ask for advice. It is in challenging times, when "management on the fly" is required, that one has an opportunity to experience the challenge, and perhaps rewards, of business ownership. Indeed, it can be a thrilling, satisfying time. But it can also be thoroughly depressing if you do not enjoy the work with the potential to ring the death knell of a business and the investment required.

BUY WHAT YOU CAN LIVE WITH: Entrepreneurs never quit working. They must be prepared to work whenever the need presents itself. Owning a business is no eight-hour-a-day job, so it must be viewed as a lifestyle that can often involve working many hours every day of the week, creating countless interruptions in one's life. But this is where the opportunity is hidden—a chance to do what others will not and rise above the pack to success of your own making, by your own rules, and to the height of your own limits.

Buy Income, Assets and a Marketing Opportunity

Often, sellers have no idea what the business they offer includes. Here is the answer: "Income, Assets and a Marketing Opportunity." This is a very convenient way to sum it up. These features are, in fact, the cornerstones of any business and precisely what is evaluated when a business valuation is performed.

INCOME = CASH FLOW: It has long been said of real estate that the secret ingredient of success is "location, location, location," and that is certainly true. With a business it's "cash flow, cash flow, cash flow," because without that a business does not survive. So it will be important to carefully reconstruct the operating statement, the business *income*, from what has been to what may be for a new owner. This prime value indicator points the way to business value and a successful acquisition.

ASSETS = SECURITY: Security in a business is created by things that make the business more than the entrepreneur in charge of management. This includes the assets—both tangible and intangible. Tangible assets, things like the fixtures, furnishings, equipment and inventory, are necessary to secure financing and, therefore, a source of wealth acquired with the business. Intangibles, such as the client contracts, employee training/benefit programs, a franchise, etc., have value, too, insofar as they contribute to the business success *without the current owner present*. Combined, tangible and intangible assets give a business the ability to take on a life of its own to form a blanket of security, hopefully resistant to the mistakes a new owner will make during the transition. When measured in terms of dollars, assets are a second prime indicator of business value.

MARKETING OPPORTUNITIES = GROWTH: There are many paths to growth. In times like these, improved results may come through mergers, where administrative and similar expenses are combined and reduced to produce a bigger net margin. But one cannot save himself into prosperity. Eventually, growth must come from increased revenue. It is important to understand and state, in very specific terms, what will be done differently [if anything] to make revenues grow before a business is acquired. The secret to making this happen is often found when evaluating marketing opportunities, or unexplored products and services to offer. This is the opportunity for a buyer to pay a price based on today's value while having a specific plan to increase results that add to value. In effect, recognizing new untapped opportunity allows one to make money when he buys.

Financing Is Not the Problem…
Good Deals Are!

Much is made of the lack of "liquidity" in economic times like these. This is a fancy way to say it's hard to get a business loan, which has a measure of truth to it. But no entrepreneur worth his or her weight in salt will permit such a thing to stand in the way when opportunity knocks. Here are several alternatives many practice to get around a lack of liquidity in times like these:

REALISTIC PRICING & VALUE: There is nothing you can do that will make a business more desirable to a buyer or a lender than creating a compelling value. Indeed, banks are awash in cash and make loans but only under the best of conditions in these times. Remember, the surest way to convince a buyer or banker to make a move on a business offered is to have a value so attractive they are both envious of your position. Provide this and the way is paved to financing.

CONSERVATIVE PLANS: Too many times buyers build their financial forecast on aggressive assumptions that incorporate growing revenue from the introduction of new business tactics. This is fine, but for purposes of financing, try assuming revenue in the coming year will *decline*. If the business still makes sense, then it is more bankable.

SELLER FINANCING: The best lender of all in uncertain times is the seller of a business. He knows it already and does not have to be convinced of its continuing viability. Plus, he may avoid capital gains tax problems by taking his sale price over several years at a good rate of interest.

SEPARATE ASSETS: Many business owners attempt to sell out "lock, stock and barrel," including the real estate. But this asset is often worth more than the business value and produces less income. A very effective way to handle this is to lease the real estate and buy the business.

PERFORMANCE BONUSES: Some business owners who cannot convince a buyer to pay their price will opt for a performance payment if the business revenue or profit continues to occur. This is usually a percentage of business results payable over one to three years.

FAMILY LOANS: A good source of financing is often found within a buyer's family. During these uncertain times, families come closer together and loans from the older to younger generations of entrepreneurs can benefit both —as fixed income for one and opportunity for the other.

BUY SMALLER: Simply stated, it could be wiser to put less money at risk and make a smaller investment. It may be possible to add, over time, more investment to make the enterprise grow. But reducing the risk to capital is always a sensible strategy to pursue.

PAY CASH: Consistent with buying a smaller business is using cash without financing to make the acquisition. Eliminating debt reduces risk dramatically, making this a very wise alternative. Paying cash for a smaller business also gives a buyer hard-hitting negating power to make money when you buy.

FIND AN EQUITY PARTNER: The woods are full of investors who want to invest in a small business. It's returns without the operating responsibility. One look at the size of the private equity industry confirms this. Seek out an investor to provide financing for a minority interest in the business. It provides highly desirable cash negotiating power to make a better deal.

Finally, in times like these, I hope the information and guidelines in this book can lead you to a better, more successful future in the small business industry.

CHAPTER I

You Value Your Business, But Can You Evaluate It?

"Good judgment comes from experience.
Experience comes from bad judgment."
—Mark Twain

When calculating indicators of business value, most mistakes are the result of inexperience. For example, the average value of a small business often exceeds $500,000. Variances of 5 to 20 percent can seem unreal or unimportant. But these translate into significant dollars, from $25,000 to $100,000. The difference between those who profit from these variances and those who don't is often experience. This is the most important benefit you receive by learning indicators of business value described in the *Business Valuation Bluebook.*

Much can be accomplished by calculating indicators of value for a business you manage, buy or sell. Do this periodically and you'll experience growing confidence that leads to improved financial results. Consider this: When you need the support of indicators of value most—an unexpected opportunity to buy or sell—will you be ready to act fast with skill, experience and good judgment?

The *Business Valuation Bluebook* describes indicators of value that can be used by business owners, entrepreneurs, business and real estate professionals and a host of others, especially "do-it-yourselfers." These solutions are easy to learn and use; plus they can provide reliable, accurate and time-saving results. They represent an alternative to lengthy and costly engagements with consultants and appraisers. Indicators of value are a valuable asset to increase your profit and wealth. Indeed, you may capture 80 percent of the benefits needed for 20 percent of the cost.

Types of Business Value

The need to know business value is frequently linked to a transfer of ownership. An entrepreneur's success or failure often depends on the ability to buy low and sell high. But how do you know where to place your bets? Those who make the most money are frequently those who understand the importance of business value best.

Business valuation can be challenging because the same company can be valued several different ways to produce a variety of results. This is because a business functions on several fields of play. The estimate is influenced by tendencies affecting the purpose of business valuation:

- Estate planners value client businesses low to minimize estate taxes.

- Bankers value businesses conservatively to limit risk when the business collateralizes a loan.

- Divorce attorneys value a business low or high depending on whom they represent.

- Business appraisers offer an unbiased opinion of value, but three appraisals on the same business are always different.

- The IRS seems to value a business low when allowing depreciation deductions and high when it is sold (to produce a bigger capital gains tax).

- Sellers want the highest price they can get while buyers want the lowest.

Who is right and who is wrong? Values that accomplish the intended objective are accepted most often as correct, so a business can have many different values at the same time. Remember, in negotiation the person with the best logic usually wins. Indicators of value provide powerful logic to support whatever position is in your best interests.

Not an Appraisal

Business appraisers perform formal business valuations. They use procedures that are more complicated and precise than the ones presented here. Developing an appraiser's level of valuation skill can take years of effort and considerable cost.

Entrepreneurs do not want or need to become business appraisers. They want to make money. Developing skill at evaluating the merits of an investment and knowing what it is worth, fast, supports this goal. Years of education to learn this skill may not be a realistic option. Moreover, given the size of many small businesses that change hands, the cost of a formal business appraisal is often a bigger solution than the problem needs. A point of diminishing return is quickly reached.

Consider Reasons and Ranges of Value

With so many reasons to calculate value, one must ask which is most appropriate for the situation. With so many indicators of value available, a "value range" can be established for any business. The one appropriate for most uses will exist somewhere within the range.

Business liquidation value is at the low end of the value range and is purely market-driven. This value is the price at which the property can be sold at auction.

Book value, another type, is constructed from assets and liabilities. This appears in every financial statement. Book value is considered very low, however, and seldom is recognized as an accurate representation of business market value.

Momentum value is another market-driven example at the upper limits of the value range. Momentum value results from a popular business concept, new technologies, impressive earnings forecasts and media attention that electrify investors. The perception of value becomes greater than the value determined from financial results. Prices can soar. Just remember to ask, "Can anyone eat a plateful of momentum?"

Benchmark indicators of value, those best suited to the entrepreneur's buying and selling activity, are derived from factors intrinsic to the business. These are cash flow, assets, returns on investment, and sales revenues. They exist in the middle of the value range and are influenced but not driven by market forces. These benchmarks take into consideration the value of intangible assets or intellectual capital, too. It is the total collection of assets deployed that builds a stream of business performance. This is projected into business value.

Business intangible assets (goodwill or intellectual capital) are what many ask about when they inquire, "What is the business goodwill worth?" Goodwill is created when business performance creates value that exceeds the fair market value of tangible assets. Goodwill is usually not as great as many think or expect. As a normal rule, goodwill is part of the indicated value—not added to the result. But there are exceptions.

Franchise value—one case in which a business does not even exist but can attract a value for goodwill is a franchise. There are thousands of franchise companies operating in the United States. They utilize imitative entrepreneurship to create the goodwill they sell. Their record of success confirms this fact. Franchisers sell a plan of success that includes a method of business operation and a uniform identity. The price paid for these benefits is a "franchise fee." It is the investment a new franchisee makes in goodwill and does not include the associated costs of starting a business: location and building improvements, furnishings, fixtures, equipment and inventory.

KEY INFORMATION

Business indicators of value are used most often when business ownership changes. This is the common ground among all who have interest in learning this skill. Accordingly, material presented throughout this text supports those professionals and entrepreneurs seeking to value businesses for this reason. Hence, the term "value" is used interchangeably with "price."

A Valuable Investment of Time

Not every indication of value needs to be extensive to provide a meaningful result. Indeed, the objective of this text is to reduce the time it takes to develop sensible estimates of business value. Million-dollar solutions are attractive but not necessary to produce a better result. The devil is in the details of discovery. Focused attention to this phase of analysis lays the groundwork for complex or simple valuation formulas. With good data, results from each type of valuation technique can be similar enough to be useful. The process does not have to be complicated—just effective.

Using business indicators of value saves time. Like most things, regular use improves skill and efficiency. With practice it is possible to calculate them for a business very quickly. Of equal importance, one discovers specific pieces of information are initial indicators of value for specific types of businesses.

The ability to identify critical information and interpret it quickly and correctly results in saving time for the entrepreneur.

KEY INFORMATION

A Diamond in the Rough

In a restaurant, cost of goods expressed as "food cost" is important. If it is out of the range of 22 to 42 percent, something is amiss. Low food cost is attractive, possibly indicating a high value. High food cost is unattractive; or it could be an opportunity in disguise—an opportunity to reduce food cost and return the savings to earnings. To discover the truth about food costs, examine three things. First, look to see if trash cans in the kitchen are full of food at the end of a business day; if so, reduce portion size. Second, ask when prices on the menu were last changed. Food costs rise periodically; retail prices must keep pace. Finally, notice how many teenagers are employed. They often eat and give away food to their friends. All three things raise food cost. Counter-measures can lower them. What you save, you keep!

Business indicators of value weed out the losers fast. For some, valuation skill helps prevent time spent on properties not worth the attention. This is not to say all businesses don't merit consideration. A "buy at the bottom" strategy suggests they do. Recognizing the right value among those with potential is the secret. When a business is sold, it includes income, assets and a marketing opportunity. The analysis encourages a review of these things. Sometimes business income is not sufficient to justify a price that is greater than the market value of the assets. This means the business price will be based on assets. Other times there will be no income at all and no assets, but an exciting marketing opportunity. These businesses are popular acquisitions: franchises. Recognizing that these components of value exist will help you direct attention to discover and evaluate the source and size of business indicators so you can measure them accurately.

Using business indicators of value saves money. This occurs when professionals can estimate value themselves. The need to hire another to perform this function is eliminated. Valuations for businesses can be quite expensive.

EFFECTIVE PHRASE

"How did you arrive at that price?"

When the business value seems too high or low, ask this question. It can completely disarm the unprepared or uninformed. If this appears to be the case, you are in a position to provide a response that will explain how value is developed and an alternative estimate. This simple strategy can win an important debate to save or earn thousands of dollars. Here's why: A solid base of logic is used to develop value. That builds confidence, which offers the strength to help one resolve issues of disagreement comfortably and favorably. Assuming both parties are equally motivated to make a deal, the side with the most logical basis supporting its position usually wins.

Business indicators of value help you buy low and sell high. The most obvious opportunity to use indicators of value and produce a direct (and favorable) impact on wealth is when buying or selling a business. At that time this skill can reduce the possibility a business will be sold for too much or too little. Sellers earn what they are worth. Buyers pay a fair price, which is important because: "You make your money when you buy—not when you sell." In either case, business indicators of value help improve the professional and financial results.

"Comps" Don't Always Compare

One doesn't have to proceed too far in a discussion of business indicators of value before rules of thumb from comparable sales show up. The premise "form follows function" is used as a best defense. For example, if 10 bowling alleys sell for an average of $35,000 per lane, then the bowling center being discussed should sell for the same multiple. What if its revenue is half or double the revenue of those in the sampling from which the multiple was developed? The use of comparable sales is suddenly suspect.

Comparable business sales, otherwise known as "comps," are often regarded as a useful device to determine business value in the buying and selling game. This is very popular in the real estate business, too, where the value of a three-bedroom ranch-style home can be determined from the recently closed sale prices of similar homes in the same neighborhood. The opportunity to compare business sales, however, is limited and less reliable. Key variables affecting this strategy are similarity of businesses in the sampling, number of businesses in the sampling, their location and the age of sale data.

Are They Similar?

Multiples from comparable sales have merit if they are created from businesses that are similar to the one under study. This means similar revenue, earnings, cash flows and operating management, which almost never occurs. The multiples are helpful as quick estimates of value but further investigation is required.

Size of sampling (number of comps) available to use is often small. This limits accuracy. No two businesses are exactly alike with the same ownership, capital structure, management skill, and market characteristics. Even like-kind franchisees that follow a proven business strategy as precisely as possible are not equal. Further, the number of businesses qualifying as suitably similar is not large. It is difficult to capture a supply of business sales data that can be used to define consistent trends with a high degree of probability.

Are They Here?

Location also affects the comparable sales when attempting to establish business indicators of value. To develop a larger database of comparable sales, many draw upon business sales data from other regions. "Casting a wider net only means the holes in the net become larger." Data taken from markets with dissimilar economic characteristics means the businesses perform differently. This unfavorably affects the quality of the information. A frozen yogurt shop in Vail, Colorado, will fetch a higher price than the same business in Nowhere, Alaska. The "location, location, location" rule always applies and affects business value.

Are They Recent?

A third weakness in the use of comps to establish value is the age of sales data. The same motive that leads a valuation consultant to seek information about sales in other locations causes them to accept information that is two, three or four years old. This type of dated information can be dangerous to use. Imagine using basic indicators of performance to value an e-commerce provider based on the companies in operation when the Internet was new. That world changed so rapidly, the value calculated would be very wrong today. Consider the effects of using comps from an area that experienced tremendous economic growth in tourism or, conversely, the layoff of thousands from major plant closings. Dated information can create inaccuracies in business value.

Comps can be helpful when their internal operating ratios are used as a device for comparison. Suppose a survey of 50 restaurants with $500,000 to $1 million in revenue reveals the average food cost is 35 percent. This can be helpful to determine how a restaurant under study compares—favorably or unfavorably—but it is not a direct indicator of business value. There are many sources for this type of information that can assist the analyst in becoming familiar with the operating characteristics of specific business types. They are not, however, strong indicators of value. Business indicators of value are developed from existing business results and market characteristics. Comps may be used to help confirm the result—but not to create it.

Valuation for Do-It-Yourselfers

Some believe calculating business indicators of value is a difficult proposition. There is a learning curve. But the potential result offers a highly favorable cost/benefit relationship. Besides that, the thickness and high cost of books on the topic tend to confirm this belief. Financial statements that provide key information only make matters worse for those with little or no exposure to accounting principles. Yet, competent business valuation is easier to learn than most realize. In fact, anyone with the ability to start, acquire, own or operate a business has all the intellectual horsepower needed. The analysis is simple and includes five steps:

1	Collect information.
2	Interpret information.
3	Reorganize information.
4	Calculate the results.
5	Put results to work.

The first three steps are a little more challenging, because they require an investment of time and effort to learn.

Surprisingly, calculating the result is the easy part, because there's little to create…just follow the directions provided in the indicators of value.

Putting results to work is the most exciting and fun part. This is where the benefits of the effort can be seen and used to buy or sell a business.

Together, these tools become the experience needed to develop good judgment.

CHAPTER 2

How to Find the Diamonds
When Mining for the Facts

When in doubt, do more research.

Study Factors That Create Value: Due Diligence

A report that describes the elements of a business that contribute to value is called a "due diligence report" or a "due diligence." This report may be a brief summary or an extensive business review and is often accompanied by descriptive exhibits. The report will describe the strengths and weaknesses of a business. Anyone can perform a due diligence but not everyone can make it meaningful. This chapter will illustrate how it can be a constructive exercise. In general, a due diligence process has two parts: discovery and interpretation.

Boundaries of a Due Diligence

Entrepreneurs must know what they are buying, selling or trading for other property. The due diligence supports this activity. It is also useful when securing financing for expansion or planning general business strategy as both are designed to improve profit. Taken a step further, the due diligence conducted to develop a business valuation is especially meaningful. A plan to increase profits by $10,000 could increase value by $50,000 or more.

Due diligence reports are prepared by business buyers, sellers, managers, independent business consultants, business or real estate brokers, bankers, accountants, attorneys, financial planners and anyone involved in business management and—the most frequent reason a due diligence is performed—ownership transfers. Settling the question of price has major financial implications.

When conducting a due diligence, the analyst collects a variety of data describing the business and its record of performance.

This is interpreted afterward and conclusions are summarized in a final report. As it may form the basis for an important decision to buy, sell or trade a business, the depth or detail of the process tends to increase in proportion to the value and commitment of money and resources.

Frequently Requested Information

The most frequently requested information for a due diligence precedent to developing indicators of value is three to five years of financial statements describing business performance. More information is also sought in follow-up requests. Following are examples of the type of materials often collected for the business valuation due diligence:

- Company identification
- Ownership structure w/shareholder agreements
- Business location and contact points
- Description of business activity
- Summary of trailing revenue, expenses and earnings
- Statement of the business capital structure (assets, liabilities, etc.)
- List of business assets
- Market position of the business
- Description of products and services offered
- Characteristics of the workforce
- Marketing opportunities within reach
- Photographs, maps and descriptions of premises and key equipment
- Location analysis
- Competitive market analysis
- A multi-year forecast of business financial results

How a Due Diligence Occurs

Collecting information for the due diligence report occurs through a series of meetings with business principals. They or their appointed representatives work closely with the analyst. These meetings expedite the due diligence/valuation process. Serious investors leave no stone unturned in their inquiries. Good information helps reduce uncertainty and reduce business risk. If transactions become lengthy, updates to the due diligence may be needed.

Performing a due diligence for a small business valued under $5 million can be difficult. Information requested is private, not public, so access has always been strictly limited. Company contacts occur directly with business principals whose sense of exposure is professional and personal. Sensitive information inadvertently released to competitors or the wrong people can cause serious damage to business performance. Financial statements are a grade card of management performance and may reveal unsatisfactory marks. Therefore, it is natural for business owners to enter a due diligence with skepticism and concern.

KEY INFORMATION

Business owners are often unwilling to disclose financial details about their business because they feel threatened. Here are actions to build trust so they will be more forthcoming with important details for the due diligence.

- Explain the benefits of a due diligence.
- Describe how the due diligence is performed.
- Ask easy, non-threatening questions first.
- Remind the owner of the objectives.
- Listen more than talk.
- Offer to execute a non-disclosure agreement.

Non-Disclosure Agreements

Non-disclosure agreements are written promises not to disclose confidential information about a business making such disclosures. General business information not considered sensitive or damaging may be released prior to execution of a non-disclosure agreement. However, the formal due diligence process begins after a non-disclosure is in place.

Those interested in learning more about a specific business—buyers, brokers, accountants, lawyers, bankers, etc.—give a non-disclosure or confidentiality agreement to the business owners. It is a normal and appropriate procedure, necessary because maintaining secrecy while conducting a due diligence is imperative to all concerned. Non-disclosure agreements permit interested parties to quickly establish their legitimacy, discretion and reliability with business principals. It is a counterpoint to a seller's release of financial information as an indication of serious intent. Non-disclosure agreements are convenient vehicles to handle this issue briskly and with dexterity.

Non-Disclosure Agreement Elements

Non-disclosure agreements are no guarantee of secrecy, however. Unfortunately, business principals themselves are often the source of information leaks. Innocent conversations with an employee, spouse or business associate may contain references that appear harmless but could be explosive. Once out of the ownership loop, "inside" information gets reinterpreted and can travel exceptionally fast. The mere mention that a due diligence is occurring may be enough to set imaginations and rumors in motion. These can demoralize employees and drive off customers. Conscientious attention to this issue by *all* parties is required to preserve confidentiality.

Non-disclosure agreements come in many forms. Some are literally an analyst's one-sentence promise not to tell what he or she learns. Others are pages of detailed instructions that converge at the point of remedies. These are threats to be carried out if the promises made are broken. Non-disclosure agreements typically include the following elements:

■ **Name of the party giving the promise:** Often names the analyst conducting the due diligence and the clients, if any.

■ **Name of the party receiving the promise**

■ **Statement of the confidentiality promise:** Explains what the analyst promises to retain as confidential (i.e., types and formats of information released). Sometimes this is added as an exhibit to ensure that specific areas are covered by the agreement while others remain off-limits. For example, material pertaining to financial performance is available, while material pertaining to product development is not. The decision to exclude certain information is most often governed by the intended use of the due diligence investigation.

15

- **Limitations on use of information received:** States the purpose for receiving privileged information. The agreement may include a statement defining who, in addition to the analyst, may have access to information disclosed. If third-party advisers—a client, supervisor, accountant, banker, attorney, business consultant, investor or other professional representative—are involved, they may be asked to execute a separate but similar agreement. This will occur prior to receipt of any privileged information.

- **Breach of the agreement:** Defines acts that constitute a breach of the agreement—generally unauthorized releases of confidential material.

- **Remedies for breach of agreement:** Typically grant the party receiving the confidentiality agreement the legal right to secure relief and compensation from the analyst. A remedy may include a provision for a restraining order and/or court injunction to prevent further release of potentially injurious information. It could also address the penalties for breach of the agreement that, in some cases, can include court costs to secure prevention of further release, cash penalties, or any other remedy legal counsel for the damaged party chooses to pursue in addition to court and legal costs of collection.

- **Term:** Normally ties expiration to a date set after the due diligence is completed; one to two years is not uncommon.

- **Signature and date**

Failure to Disclose Is a Deal-Killer

In some cases, despite the existence of a fully executed confidentiality agreement, business principals may elect to withhold certain information requested. This may be ownership's prerogative. Confidentiality agreements do not necessarily grant the analyst rights to demand information; they grant business principals the right to take legal action if information disclosed is not kept confidential. Still, failing to disclose relevant information can be a warning flag. It may also be counterproductive, as it prevents the analyst from conducting a due diligence in advance of a business valuation. Worse, it often creates suspicion that business principals are attempting to cover up problematic issues. Business buyers or their representatives will usually withdraw their interest when information is withheld.

EFFECTIVE PHRASE

"Would you ever buy a business sight unseen?"

This is a formidable response to the owner that says, "Bring me an offer and I'll show you my books." This frequently heard statement is a common response among owners threatened by inquiries about their business. Developing a meaningful business value without data, however, forces the valuation consultant to work blindfolded—an unrealistic expectation.

The Primary Asset of a Business

The primary asset purchased with a business is usually the stream of income. Without financial records to describe it, neither broker nor buyer can know what is offered. The broker attempting to represent a property with undocumented benefits is playing a high-risk game. Any investor attempting to buy it is exposed to high levels of uncertainty. Both make commitments of time and money to investigate a risk-filled venture without knowing if initial interest or effort is justified. Neither can calculate an initial estimate of value based on fact.

Perhaps more importantly, accountants or attorneys cannot properly advise the parties as to the size and scope of business implications created by a business transaction without detailed disclosures. Nor will bankers consider financing any kind of business without financial disclosures to justify and assure that repayment of debt is plausible. The ability to repay from business earnings must be clear and unquestionable. This is possible only when financial disclosures (limited, while still revealing enough to engender increased interest) are made at the appropriate time—before the offer is made.

The non-disclosure agreement is a precedent to a due diligence. This comes before an offer to purchase a business that spells out the conditions of a sale. A contract contingency to permit more detailed disclosures after acceptance of an initial offer is the norm. Experienced brokers perform their due diligence when listing a property in anticipation of questions and inquiries that will follow. They know a client's follow-up investigation will occur to confirm the specifics of representations.

Business owners who fail to disclose necessary information as part of a due diligence investigation are shortsighted. They immediately disqualify knowledgeable and capable players. The price paid is very often a business that does not sell, becomes shop-worn or becomes known as "on the market" over time. It can be weakened by competitors and eventually lose customers and business revenue. Ownership burnout often occurs, as well. The final outcome may be liquidation for pennies on the dollar. Sadly, with a good due diligence/business valuation and reasonable expectations, such a business might have sold earlier for a profit.

To ensure that business principals are cooperative and forthcoming with information needed, add a failure to disclose provision to the confidentiality agreement. As a result, requested materials are easier to collect. If materials are not forthcoming, the analyst may be released from any continuing obligation to perform services.

Organizing a Due Diligence

Knowing what to ask, when to ask for it and how to organize information will make a due diligence easier and more productive. It is helpful to recall two premises that prompt the effort: 1) Is information related to a specific event? (Does someone want to buy, sell, trade or refinance the business?) and 2) Is the due diligence related to a specific time? (How much time is going to be available to complete the task?)

Suppose owners of a restaurant were interested in financing to expand the kitchen production capacity—an event. Indicators needed for a quick feasibility estimate might include the following:

- Financial statements
- Existing mortgages or liens
- Leases for equipment and the location
- Current equipment list with descriptions of major machinery
- A three-year revenue/earnings forecast

This should be sufficient to construct a preliminary cost/benefit assessment of the proposed expansion strategy. If favorable, a more complete due diligence may be performed. From that, indicators of value are calculated to measure the total benefit of the expansion plan. Sometimes adding $10,000 to earnings creates an additional $50,000 of business value indicated—equity. Keep this in mind. Bankers want to know how much additional profit is created, but using indicators of business value permits the entrepreneur to go farther by estimating wealth created through refinancing to support expansion.

Expect the Unexpected

The opportunity to buy or sell a business is frequently unexpected. For this reason, time is a factor when information to produce indicators of value is needed fast. Perhaps an opportunity to acquire a competitor or accept an unsolicited offer is in play. The more likely approach to a due diligence in this case will begin with an all-out document dump. Everything comes at once and it is the analyst's job to quickly organize, prioritize and produce meaningful results.

The value of calculating indicators of business value periodically is revealed when opportunity comes unexpectedly as it so often does. Acting fast and with confidence provides a competitive advantage.

To simplify the reporting process, data may be prioritized in categories. This divides discovery into steps that match the results needed with the time and energy expended to develop them.

Follow receipt of initial indicators of business performance by requesting other key variables and strings of more detailed data. This would be priority types of information from other categories within the due diligence inquiry. For example, food cost information is more meaningful when combined with traffic count at the existing location, seating capacity and service style, market position, promotional tactics, age of kitchen and equipment and menu selections. One or two descriptive sentences for each is often enough to determine if the property is worth a closer look. If the initial impressions are not attractive, move on—wasting little time.

 KEY INFORMATION

Here's a helpful shortcut. Restaurateurs are acutely aware of *food cost* (i.e., the cost of food purchased expressed as a percent of gross income). This data item offers a quick indicator of gross profitability. If the figure is low, management probably runs a tight ship; too high and there are probably old prices on the menu, excessive waste in the garbage at day's end, or theft. This single measurement device provides valuable clues to the restaurant's overall operating efficiency. Determine this percentage of revenue first.

Checklists Lead to the Next Step

To organize and prioritize information efficiently, the checklists (covering Finance, Control, Marketing, Sales, Production and Service) in Appendix C may be helpful. These categories are common to all businesses, and the information listed can be selected on a case-by-case basis. Asterisked (*) items are most important as they help form a good early impression of the business with less due diligence.

The Sergeant Said

To see your target in the dark,
It often helps to set your mark
In line of sight just to the right:
Then your bulls-eye comes to light.
—Warren Lane Molton

CHAPTER 3

Reading Business History— Balance Sheets

Accurate variables produce reliable values.

Calculating indicators of business value is not possible without key variables. Selecting accurate variables, not completing a math equation, determines the quality of the result. It is possible with business financial records that are the source of most data retrieved from a due diligence. Always use data from the past three to five years. Selected information catches the eye of the business valuation consultant. Some data will be used in their original form while others are reconstituted for greater meaning. When accurately extracted, developed and introduced into valuation formulas, they can create reliable business values.

Business Balance Sheet

A financial statement uses numbers to describe the business capital structure. The financial statement has two basic parts:

■ **The balance sheet,** which includes a list of business assets and liabilities (essence of the capital structure)

■ **The operating statement,** which is a record of business revenue, expenses and earnings

Consider the Balance Sheet

Assets

The first variables to identify describe the value of assets included in a business. The two measures of asset value to identify

23

are book value of assets and their fair market value (FMV). Both are affected, increased or decreased, by several factors.

A list of assets appears in the first or top section of the balance sheet. Assets are divided into two categories. These are **current assets** that include such things as cash-on-hand, accounts receivable, prepaid expenses, certain types of equipment, and inventory. The second category includes larger items such as land and buildings, which are considered **fixed assets**.

The value assigned to each asset listed is taken from its original cost when placed in service (acquired for use by the business). Also listed is an entry called "accumulated depreciation." This is a deduction representing a loss of asset value resulting from normal wear-and-tear in use. The amount of depreciation taken is subtracted from the asset's original cost. Asset values and accumulated depreciation are often grouped together for simplicity. The difference between original cost of assets and depreciation subtracted is the "book" value of business assets—their value as they appear in the business books.

 EFFECTIVE PHRASE

"You get income, assets and a marketing opportunity."

Say the above when a buyer asks, "If I buy this business, what do I get for my money?" It's a short response that opens the door for arguments designed to justify business value. Many of the benefits of business ownership are intangible. But these fall short of the inquiry of the steely-eyed buyer preparing to write a check. Most want to know they are acquiring "tangible" assets in exchange for cash. They are, in fact, acquiring both tangibles and intangibles.

Tangible vs. Intangible Assets

Frequently, the only assets listed in a financial statement are tangible—property one can touch and feel. Typically, intangible assets are not included in the asset variable used to value the business. They differ because they cannot be touched or directly felt. Likewise, banks do not accept intangible assets as collateral for financing. Exceptions may occur, however, when intangible assets are directly connected to revenue creation. Patents, copyrights, secret formulas or production processes are common examples. These can be listed in the balance sheet summary of assets. The final estimate of asset value will be used in the excess earnings and leveraged cash flow formulas presented in chapters dealing with those valuation techniques.

Goodwill

In some cases goodwill is listed as an intangible asset. Confusion may surround the meaning of "goodwill" when the term is used to represent value in a business. In many cases an investor, acting on the advice of a professional representative, will refuse to pay for goodwill as a part of the business price. The implication is that goodwill is intangible; therefore, conveying nothing of value and not a fair exchange for cash or property. The real intent, though, may be to avoid allocating any portion of the purchase price to goodwill. This is because goodwill, according to the Internal Revenue Code, is amortized in a particular manner. It offers limited tax benefits compared to other assets with shorter, or more favorable, depreciation or amortization periods.

EFFECTIVE PHRASE

"Goodwill is the excess of purchase price for a business over the market value of its tangible assets."

This is the quick response to the often-asked question, "What's my goodwill worth?" The response is provided by the Internal Revenue Code. It's a deflection from a more meaningful response but one that is necessary. It is not possible to estimate the value of goodwill without estimating the value of the business. This approach buys time and shifts the discussion to the need for more information. Use it as an opportunity to explain why a simple due diligence (review of financial records) is needed. Explain that goodwill is not valued separately from the business, or without the total business value. Instead, value the business first, subtract the value of tangibles and the remainder is the intangibles—goodwill (to their way of thinking). Close the discussion with, "I'll be happy to estimate the value of your goodwill once I estimate the value of your business."

Where goodwill is justifiable, it is not difficult to illustrate its value. Compare the cost to buy the benefits of goodwill (revenue, earnings, reputation, location, market position, procedures and product/service mix) with the investment required to build it (and the accompanying benefits) from scratch. Also, consider the time it takes to buy versus build. Keep in mind the risk to a start-up business is often much greater than the risk of failure in a business already performing successfully. Sometimes buying goodwill is a good deal.

Obsolescence

This term indicates an asset, service or product that is becoming obsolete and losing its value. It is important to recognize obsolescence because it will affect, favorably or unfavorably, the value of business assets. Old inventory not suitable for resale, for example, or equipment no longer in use, might be discounted (perhaps below book value) when attempting to estimate tangible business asset values. Two kinds of obsolescence are important to consider.

Functional obsolescence occurs when the need or demand for an asset ceases to exist. For example, printing presses will become obsolete as demand for documents transmitted via email and the Internet grows. Newspapers and magazines are published electronically. This eliminates the cost of paper, printing and shipping, offering publishers a significant savings of manpower, time and money. The increased speed of production shortens the information cycle so the product timeliness and desirability improves, too. Books published directly on the Internet will contribute further to the growing obsolescence of printing presses.

Economic obsolescence is another way assets become obsolete. This often occurs in tandem with its functional cousin. Declining demand for older computer microprocessors is related to new software that would run only on faster, more powerful chips (functional obsolescence). Consequently, sales and the economic value of older chips are constantly being eliminated. This is economic obsolescence.

Economic obsolescence may also occur independently, however. A good example is found in a business's heating and cooling system (HVAC). Significant improvements of energy efficiencies in HVAC equipment have occurred in the past decade. Compared to old systems, new units do a better job managing air in the workplace environment. They also create savings, permitting their cost to be recovered in a few years. As a result, many business owners discover that, while still functional, old systems are too expensive to operate. Economic obsolescence has occurred and the value of the affected equipment is reduced.

Consider Appreciation

In some instances appreciation will cause an asset's value to exceed its book value. Simple marketplace growth is a common reason. A building might have appreciated in value because of market trends even though it is being depreciated for tax purposes. Real estate values in good locations usually rise. Thus, original cost and book values are lower than the price investors would pay to acquire such a resource. In the alternative, an accelerated depreciation schedule may outpace the useful life of an asset to create a similar disparity between book and economic value.

Appreciation may also occur when an asset value can be increased due to a unique/specific function—its highest and best use. For example, mobile home communities often purchase and rent used mobile homes. These are aggressively depreciated but can remain useful for many years. Suppose the rent collectable is $350 per month. Using the capitalization method of business valuation and a 50 percent rate of return, the economic value of a single mobile home rental might be $8,400. The book value, however, could be zero.

Because the book value of each asset can be affected by functional or economic obsolescence, or appreciation, making appropriate adjustments in asset values improves accuracy of the business valuation estimate.

Market & Replacement Value

Market value is the amount one could reasonably expect to pay for an asset. It may be synonymous with replacement value or the cost to replace an asset with another of like kind. Neither reflects a property's book value nor its original cost—they usually lie somewhere between the two. It may be difficult to develop a value estimate in which all agree. Use original cost, book value, appraisals (if available) and discussions with ownership or knowledgeable industry professionals to develop a reasonable estimate of market or replacement asset values. More cooks will not spoil the stew.

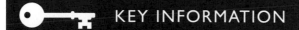

KEY INFORMATION

When all is said and done, lenders tend to rely on book value as the basis for conservative loan approvals. Sellers want to use original or current economic value to raise the business price. Buyers try to use economic value to borrow and book value to buy. The analyst's job is to develop a complete set of defensible key variables, including book, market and replacement asset values. It will be used in the valuation formulas.

Liabilities

Following the list of assets on a balance sheet is a list of the business's debts, or liabilities. These are categorized as current or long-term. The former includes obligations such as accounts payable, operating lines of credit due within 90 days, accrued vacation pay, and so on. The latter typically includes loans secured to purchase the business, related property and equipment, or major capital improvements. Sometimes loans to shareholders will appear in this section. The current and long-term liabilities are combined to indicate the total liabilities of a business.

Equity

Subtracting existing debt from the net value of capital and property (which in some cases includes intellectual capital) contributed to an investment yields the equity amount. Ownership equity *in an acquisition* is usually the down payment used to acquire a business. This is called "hard" equity because it represents a commitment of physical resources (e.g., cash). This does not always occur in a business acquisition, however. Some businesses are purchased wholly with borrowed funds, so there is no equity.

How, then, can equity be created where there is no original investment? Four forces combine to produce equity: income, tax benefits, amortization and appreciation.

1. Income: Without spending a dime for equity, it is possible to get a job and make a living wage. Ownership of a business should offer this, too, or the investment is questionable.

2. Tax Benefits: Businesses have the potential to offer tax savings on earnings compared with the same earnings provided by a job. Some businesses have deductions that reduce the earnings they create. The effect is to reduce taxable earnings and tax liability but not necessarily cash flow. Consequently, employment and business earnings could be the same, but the latter might be taxed at a lower marginal rate. A tax savings can be the result.

3. Amortization: Business ownership can be like an investment savings account. With reasonable financial leverage and effective management, payment on debt comes from business earnings. A portion of each payment on the debt is credited to interest on the outstanding loan. The remainder retires the principal until the debt is fully paid. Each principal payment represents a reduction in debt and, provided the business has not declined in value, a corresponding increase in ownership equity.

4. Appreciation: When a business appreciates, its value grows. Business revenue and earnings increase because of effective management, favorable market forces and a variety of other reasons. Normally, increases in earnings are translated into greater business value, and the increase becomes added equity for ownership.

The combination of income, tax benefits, amortization and appreciation has an effect on ownership equity similar to compounding. Many underestimate the total effect magnified by an improved ability to buy low and sell high.

In addition to hard equity, there is another type called "sweat equity"—created by entrepreneurs with the management skill to run a business successfully. If the business grows in value, additional equity is the result. Management entrepreneurs can receive stock or ownership in lieu of a portion of their salary or in the place of bonuses. This is normal and accompanied by performance measurements to ensure stock is not given freely. Unlike hard equity, this form comes from a commitment of time, talent and energy. It can provide a convenient way for entrepreneurs to acquire a business interest with nothing down.

The amount of equity in a business can affect its value. Businesses with little or no debt are sometimes perceived as more stable and secure. Absence of debt suggests a business that can withstand changes in sales cycles, capitalize on unexpected market opportunities, compensate employees well and show little or no deferred maintenance or obsolescence in furnishings and equipment. This perception of security may generate a premium value compared to businesses burdened by heavy debt—provided the absence of debt is not accompanied by a sense of complacency on the part of management.

Sometimes a section of the balance sheet shows a reconciliation of *stockholder* or *owner's equity*. This is not the same as the business's value. It is also not a measurement of equity based on the business value estimate but, instead, is benchmarked against the book value. (Business book value is the book value of all assets minus liabilities.)

Generally, owner's equity is a function of cash paid for the business or stock in the company, additional cash paid into the company, and earnings that have been allowed to remain in the business (called *retained earnings*). The owner's equity portion of the balance sheet also describes the amount of stock the company is authorized to issue, the par (nominal or face) value of each share and the number of shares outstanding.

"In business, numbers are the symbols by which you measure the various activities of an individual enterprise. They are not the business; they are only pictures of the business. Numbers serve as a sort of thermometer which measures the health and well-being of the enterprise."
—Hal Geneen

Penetrating the persona of a business through its numbers improves understanding of business capacity, problems and potential.

BALANCE SHEET
BELL-Quest, Ltd.

ASSETS
Current Assets

Inventory at Cost	$ 55,000.00
Accounts Receivable	13,498.41
Prepaid Expenses	2,401.08
Security Deposits	675.00
Cash in Accounts	19,904.66
Furnishings and Equipment	15,000.00
Accumulated Depreciation	<15,000.00>
Net Current Assets	$ 91,479.15

Fixed Assets

Land @ Cost	$ 7,500.00
Building	80,000.00
Accumulated Depreciation	<29,333.00>
Net Building	50,667.00
Intangibles and Goodwill	25,000.00
Accumulated Amortization	<18,333.00>
Net Intangibles and Goodwill	6,667.00
Net Fixed Assets	$ 64,834.00
TOTAL ASSETS	$156,313.15

LIABILITIES
Current Liabilities

Accounts Payable	$ 33,127.50
Expenses Due	7,638.00
Operating Credit Line	0.00
Employee Benefits/Taxes Payable	542.88
Total Current Liabilities	$ 41,308.38

Long-Term Liabilities

Bank Loan on Business	$ 49,323.13
TOTAL LIABILITIES	90,631.51
OWNERSHIP EQUITY	65,681.64
TOTAL LIABILITIES AND EQUITY	$156,313.15

CHAPTER 4

Reading Business History— Profit & Loss Statements

Cash flow analysis for the math impaired.

Contrary to popular belief, calculating indicators of business value is not rocket science. Simple math skills are often enough. Indeed, most already have 100 percent of the skills needed and 90 percent of the information. Ten percent of reorganizing this data is all that remains. Substantial benefits are available for those willing to make a small investment of effort to learn these techniques.

Profit & Loss Statement

The second part of the financial statement describes business revenue, expenses, and profit or loss created from operations. This document provides the most important data needed to develop a coherent business value.

In general, it offers a description of the business results for the current and previous years. There are many names for a summary of a business's record of financial performance. To name a few:

- Books
- Profit and Loss Report
- Operating Statement
- EOY (End of Year) Results
- P&L
- Income Summary

How to Proceed

To construct indicators of business value, copy data from this section of the financial statement onto a standard form profit & loss statement. This is a detailed but valuable exercise. When copying data the entrepreneur's attention is directed to each entry. Besides speeding up familiarity with the business, it also will prompt important questions for management to consider such as, "How was [an expense] created?" or "Why is [an item] increasing or decreasing?" and "Is [a certain expense] necessary to operate the business?" Asking such questions prior to performing a valuation exercise frequently unearths new data to offer a clearer picture of the business's earning power.

Placing financial data into a familiar format has other benefits, too. Familiarity reduces difficulty. This is important since business financial statements are constructed in a variety of formats. Using the same format with each new analysis makes the job easier. In addition, forms presented in this text highlight key data linked to valuation formulas that follow. When transferring data to the analyst's forms, certain items will appear that are common to most businesses. A discussion of those items follows.

Revenue

Revenue is created by the sale of a business's products or services. Gross income does not include revenue from sources unrelated to the principal business activity (e.g., interest on bank deposits owned by the business, earnings or rents from investments made and owned by the business, etc.). Observe the trend of revenue during previous years, taking note of significant increases or decreases. Attempt to correlate trends with specific events related to management or the marketplace—therein lies the reason they may have occurred, providing valuable insight into business planning.

Cost of Goods

"Cost of goods" represents the total wholesale cost of merchandise purchased or produced for resale. In retailing, distributing or wholesaling, business items purchased are sold at a higher price. In a restaurant, cost of goods is often referred to as "food cost" or the cost of bulk food purchased to produce the meals served. Manufacturing businesses include the cost of raw materials and labor required to build the finished product in their cost of goods calculations.

How to Calculate Cost of Goods

Calculate cost of goods by subtracting from revenue the cost of all merchandise purchased during the year. Take a second step and examine cost of goods as a percent of revenue, as this can be revealing. In times of increasing business activity, cost of goods as a percent of revenue might remain fixed or decrease slightly. Increases in the percent of cost of goods may accompany declining revenues—business might be slow. Inventory taken for owners' use is another reason cost of goods could increase. Anticipation of a business sale is another. Poor cash flows that restrict the ability to maintain inventory at optimum levels also accompany falling revenues.

Gross Profit

This is revenue left after cost of goods has been subtracted. When calculating a product's retail price from its wholesale cost, the percent of markup is added to the wholesale price. Suppose an item costs ten dollars ($10.00) and the markup for resale is 50 percent. One would take 50 percent of $10.00 ($5.00) and add it to the cost of the product ($10.00), resulting in a sales price of $15.00. But be aware that while the markup is 50 percent, the gross margin (gross profit when stated as a percent of the retail price instead of wholesale cost) is 33 percent. The latter percentage is calculated by dividing the resale price into the amount of markup ($5÷$15). It is important to differentiate between markup and margin in conversation. Here's why:

KEY INFORMATION

A Shortcut to Cash Flow

First impressions of business profitability can be created from three simple questions.

1. What is the average revenue per month?
2. What is the average markup on merchandise or services?
3. What are the average operating costs per month?

Divide the average monthly revenue by 1 + the percent of markup on merchandise sold. The answer is the cost of goods per month. Subtract this amount from revenue to determine gross profit. Subtract monthly expenses from gross profit. The answer is an estimate of business cash flow. Sample monthly performance below.

Revenue @ $50,000 / 130% Cost of Goods = $38,461.54

Revenue - $38,461.54 = $11,538.46 Gross Profit

Gross Profit @ $11,538.46 - $6,000 Expenses = $5,538.46 Net

$5,538.46 Net Monthly X 12 = $66,461.53 Annual Net Profit

Next, determine if the business's earning power justifies continued interest. If so, the due diligence that follows will attempt to confirm these initial conclusions.

Another situation occurs in which understanding ways to calculate gross revenue from cost of goods, and the inverse, is helpful. This is when taking a business inventory prior to the sale of a company. It is necessary to determine how much inventory is present and included in the sale price. The physical inventory is typically taken by an outside inventory service that counts all the merchandise based on retail price. This method is faster than checking thousands of items against their original invoiced costs.

KEY INFORMATION

A Shortcut to the Closing Table

Suppose inventory is marked up 30 percent and has a retail value of $75,000. By subtracting 30 percent from $75,000, the indicated wholesale value could be $52,500. But this is wrong! Thirty percent of the expected resale price is more than 30 percent of the actual cost of goods. The retail value is 130 percent of the cost of goods. Therefore, when the retail value ($75,000) is divided by 130 percent, the actual wholesale value of the inventory is $57,692.31…$5,192 more!

Operating Expenses

All the costs of running a business are the business expenses. They include insurance, payroll, depreciation, interest, maintenance, rent, office supplies, freight, automobile and travel expenses, and so forth. Keep two things in mind when reviewing a business's record of expenses.

First Scenario

"You can't save yourself into prosperity." Tom Woods, former Chief Financial Officer of TWA notes this when responding to management preoccupied with cost cutting strategies. Frugality may be a virtue but it is possible to take a good thing too far. Cost cutting, in the extreme, translates into declining production capacity and the ability to serve demands from existing and potential customers. Thus begins a vicious cycle.

Reductions in expenses are not too difficult to make. They will, however, increase the workload and stress on existing employees and resources needed to fill the gap they create. If not restored to previous levels, production and service may decline. Sales will likely decrease. This causes more expense reductions, which is the cycle renewing itself in a business that is slowly bleeding to death.

A classic example of this scenario occurs when the budget ax hits marketing, advertising and training budgets in response to poor revenue. Revenue and brand awareness go hand in hand. Indeed, in these days of electronic commerce, the "brand" floating in cyberspace is often all the customer knows. So market awareness and revenue have become inseparable. It is good to remember that cutting expenses is a short-term fix and a finite strategy to improve profitability. Keeping the focus on ways to increase revenue has infinite possibilities and, though painful in the short term, can insure long-term prosperity.

Second Scenario

The second characteristic of expenses is that business owners intentionally maximize them to minimize earnings and tax liability. Therefore, a thorough review of expenses is a valuable prerequisite to the business valuation steps. Upon review, expenses, notskimming, can be a source of cash flow not readily apparent in the business's net profit.

Net Profit

Subtracting expenses from gross profit calculates earnings, known as "net profit," "net operating income," "NOI," "profit," "taxable income," or simply "earnings" and so on. Typically, net profit is stated after depreciation, amortization and interest, as well as all other business expenses, are deducted.

In conversation with others, it is important to define precisely what net profit really means. Different people have different ideas, and confusion can be costly. When allowed to continue, such misunderstandings can hinder the valuation process and negatively affect its intended use thereafter.

Earnings Summary

An earnings summary is a short form of the business operating (income and expense) statement. It will include the basic key variables just mentioned: gross revenue, cost of goods, gross profit, expenses and net profit.

EARNINGS SUMMARY BELL-Quest, Ltd.	
Revenue	$ 608,951.00
Cost of Goods	<390,190.00>
Gross Profit	218,761.00
Expenses	<189,501.29>
Net Profit	29,260.00

These, or variants of each, appear in most business operating statements. The earnings summary helps simplify the problem of becoming acquainted quickly with a business operating statement. Look for the earnings summary to simplify the investigation.

Trailing Earnings

Trailing earnings are earnings recorded during previous years of business operation. These are important because they represent the rock-hard reality of a business's performance—not its potential. Indicators of value are more often based on trailing earnings and not a forecast of blazing success. Remember, history remains the best predictor of future performance. Consider three to five years of trailing earnings when constructing business indicators of value.

Examining trailing earnings is also important because businesses are in a constant state of change. Calculating indicators of value from one year of performance does not take into consideration business trends. These could be highly favorable or unfavorable, thereby affecting the conclusion.

For this reason, use trailing earnings as a way to introduce the influence of trends into estimates of business value. For the sophisticated entrepreneur, trailing earnings trends provide the basis for forecasting future earnings. For most, however, trailing earnings are useful to weigh cash flows that already exist and influence variables used in creating a risk/price multiple, described in the next chapter. Study the operating statement that follows.

PROFIT & LOSS STATEMENT
BELL-Quest, Ltd.   January 1 thru December 31

REVENUE	
Gross Sales	$ 581,282.00
Service Income	27,669.00
Total Revenue	$ 608,951.00
COST OF GOODS	
Merchandise Purchases	$ 339,439.00
Labor on Service	$ 20,751.00
Total Cost of Goods	<$ 390,190.00 >
GROSS PROFIT	$ 218,761.00
EXPENSES	
Advertising	35,913.50
Amortization	1,667.66
Auto & Truck	332.00
Commissions	6,187.12
Depreciation	4,809.00
Dues & Subscriptions	179.00
Entertainment	1,776.00
Freight	11,378.60
Insurance	2,835.00
Interest	4,533.29
Janitorial	3,882.00
Laundry & Uniforms	900.00
Licenses	75.00
Non-Recurring Expenses	501.66
Payroll	61,871.22
Payroll Taxes	4,604.34
Professional Fees	900.00
Real Estate Taxes	5,743.00
Repairs & Maintenance	2,700.00
Salaries (Owner's)	18,000.00
Supplies Office	421.00
Travel	1,487.53
Telephone	2,964.00
Utilities	12,828.00
Other	3,012.37
Total Expenses	$ 189,501.29
NET PROFIT	$ 29,259.71

CHAPTER 5

Net Profit Versus Cash Flow

It's not what you make—it's what you keep.

Variables used with indicators of business value are retrieved from the data secured when the due diligence is performed. These variables are not particularly difficult to develop, but maintaining accuracy is very important. For example, cash flow is the base variable from which indicators of value are constructed. If they are incorrect, results can be off the mark. This can be very costly. Take great care when building these indicators of value. Small adjustments may correctly or incorrectly magnify the outcome.

Net Profit or Cash Flow?

Recall obsolescence affects the value of business assets. Depending on the particular situation, an asset could be worth more or less than its book value. Adjust asset values to account for obsolescence that may have occurred. Similarly, an earnings reconstruction (ERCON) resolves discrepancies between apparent and actual business earnings. To do this, add expenses [to the net profit] of the current owner that will not exist or be different for a new owner.

The ERCON is performed after the analyst has become familiar with the business's financial statements. With the ERCON, key variables may be developed: EBIT (Earnings Before Interest and Taxes), EBITDA (Earnings Before Income Taxes, Depreciation & Amortization), cash flow, free cash flow and more. These are used as variables with indicator of value formulas: capitalizing income; multiple of excess earnings; levering cash flow into equity and debt.

An ERCON is necessary because business owners frequently maximize expenses to minimize earnings. This is a strategy of tax avoidance used to limit taxable earnings so tax liability may be reduced. It is also a catch-22. To the untrained or inexperienced, the business net profit may not seem appealing and makes a business investment less attractive. This situation is the real reason most owners resist financial disclosures to potential buyers of their business.

Simply put, business net profit will seldom justify a realistic business value compared to those derived from business cash flow or free cash flow. An owner knows the difference between what is reported for tax purposes and what he or she actually gets to keep. Explaining it to a buyer is a challenge. But when access to financial details of a business is denied, an ERCON and subsequent valuations cannot be completed. So, ownership's tax avoidance strategy becomes an albatross around their neck. It can prevent them from adequate justifications of value. Resolving the issue enables parties involved to see clearly how a selected business value can be justified. EBIT and EBITDA are popular examples of variables produced using the simplest type of ERCON. Many business professionals regularly use these terms.

EBIT & EBITDA

EBIT is an acronym that means Earnings Before Interest and Taxes. In this case earnings are synonymous with net profit. To calculate EBIT, add the business's interest expense to the net profit. If income taxes are treated as an expense or a deduction before net profit is calculated, add it, too. Note, however, these types of taxes are normally subtracted after net profit is calculated. When one or both of these costs are added to net profit, the resulting value is called EBIT.

EBITDA is EBIT on steroids and includes expenses called Depreciation and Amortization. These values may be added to the net profit because no cash is paid out for depreciation or amortization. The acronym therefore represents Earnings Before Income Taxes, Depreciation & Amortization.

The IRS takes the position that investments in tangible and certain intangible assets may be recovered over time by the taxpayer. The vehicle used to accomplish this is a prorated share of their original value charged as an expense to the business operation. This is a substitute for treating the original cost as an expense in the first year the asset was acquired. Consequently, since the original cost was paid in the beginning, the amount expensed each year does not represent cash paid out. It is, therefore, a deduction only and may be added back to EBIT. The resulting variable, EBITDA, is often considered a more accurate reflection of business earnings available to ownership. The variance between net profit and cash flow grows.

Depreciation

Certain assets used in the production of business income can be deducted from gross revenue either directly or indirectly. This is how the Internal Revenue Service enables business owners to recover the cost of assets purchased by the business, hence the alternative name: "cost recovery."

Direct expense deductions include cost of goods, rent and other items such as office supplies. Indirect deductions occur when an asset's useful life extends beyond a typical business period (one year). In these cases a portion of the asset's value is deducted each year to represent the gradual wasting away of the asset that occurs. When fully depreciated, an asset's book value can be zero. To determine the actual amount of depreciation that can be taken, check current IRC regulations.

Some assets cannot be depreciated. Personal assets, a home or a car not used for business are examples. Other assets with an indefinite life, such as land, are not depreciated either.

Amortization

Amortization is the depreciation of intangible assets. It appears as a deduction in the expense section of a business operating statement. Unlike their tangible counterparts, intangible assets are amortized according to a different schedule. The typical amortization period is 15 years—straight line. In all cases, check the current IRC regulations for rules regarding use of amortization.

In the past the IRC has indicated amortization applies to assets acquired by the business that are actively used to produce income. It does not indicate intangibles created by the business that can be amortized. However, in certain cases assets such as copyrights and patents that have been shown to have definite limited lives may be amortized.

Examples of intangible assets that might be amortized are goodwill and other intangibles purchased, start-up costs, organization costs, research and experimental costs, a covenant not to compete, patents, copyrights, and customer lists. Amortization expenses are added to business earnings to complete the variable: <u>EBITDA</u>. This is a more accurate indicator of the business's earning power. A sample earnings reconstruction below shows EBITDA is 37.6 percent greater than net profit.

EARNINGS RECONSTRUCTION
BELL-Quest, Ltd.

Revenue	$ 608,951
Cost of Goods	<$ 390,190>
Gross Profit	$ 218,761
Expenses	<$ 189,501>
Net Profit	$ 29,260
Interest	$ 4,533
Taxes	-----
EBIT	$ 33,793
Depreciation	$ 4,809
Amortization	$ 1,668
EBITDA	$ 40,270

Cash Flow

Although depreciation and amortization are two widely accepted additions to business earnings, there are others. These can be related to the future use of the business, a change in management strategy or sale of the business. Identify new expenses that do not exist under the present circumstances that could increase or decrease EBITDA. These adjustments, positive and negative, are added or subtracted from EBITDA to identify a business "cash flow" that is often greater still. It is earnings available to ownership following the expected change in business strategy or ownership, provided the previous year's business results remain unchanged. Cash flow is important.

Weighted Cash Flow

There can be occasions when use of one year's cash flow increases investment risk. A weighted cash flow is helpful when a business is experiencing strong growth trends or downturns in results. This device will diminish the influence of trends on business cash flow and is used as a replacement for one year's cash flow. This approach is less aggressive but it remains reliable, thereby reducing risk to the investor.

To calculate a weighted cash flow, the current year and the previous one or two years of operating statements are used. An ERCON is performed with each year. Thereafter, a weighting scale is used. When using the current and one previous year, the current year cash flow is multiplied by two and added to the previous year. Then, divide the result by three to produce a cash flow estimate weighted two-to-one in favor of the current year.

EFFECTIVE PHRASE

"Buy my business sight-unseen!"

That's what business owners say to buyers when they refuse to make financial records available. Revealing revenue, expenses, net profit and even cash flow is how one evaluates the key benefits offered by the business and making the investment to buy it. Without this data it would be difficult, if not impossible, to justify any business value.

When three years of results are used, multiply the current year's cash flow by three, the previous year's cash flow by two and add cash flow from the earliest year. Divide the combined result by six to produce a cash flow that bears a 3:2:1 weighting. Again, current trends are given greater emphasis but not used exclusively for the valuation analysis.

"Perks"
Positive Adjustments to Earnings

Perks are several types of expenses that may be added in part or entirely to earnings. Many will fall into the following categories: education, employee benefits, entertainment, home office, interest, non-recurring expenses, payroll, transportation and travel—in addition to depreciation and amortization. The discussion that assumes deductions for certain expenses is allowed by IRC guidelines.

Taxation rules and regulations are sometimes warped beyond recognition by ownership pursuing an aggressive tax avoidance strategy. They are further complicated by the frequent changes in the IRS code. Justification for certain expenses provides the basis for adjustment—addition to earnings. Conference with professional representatives of the business and, <u>in all cases</u>, review the current IRC rules to determine what adjustments are, and are not, allowable. Nothing provided in this text overrules the current IRS code, which is the final authority. The following is a list of generally recognized adjustments.

Education

Education expenses might be deducted provided the purpose of the education is deemed required or necessary for the pursuit of business activity. Generally, if the education is needed to improve business skills or meet legal or licensing requirements, it is deductible.

It is fairly easy to imagine a situation where a buyer with considerable experience is acquiring a business. Education expenses for employees of the previous owner may no longer be necessary; thus, these could be considered additions to earnings.

Employee Benefits

Employee benefits are paid to employees of the business who receive compensation. The most common form of employee benefit is insurance. Medical insurance is costly, and premiums paid to a departing owner may be considered cash flow if not reassigned to a new owner. The same can be said of life insurance used to fund an estate, or company contributions to a pension plan. If not to be paid to new ownership, these are adjustments to earnings.

Entertainment

Entertaining clients in the course of business is a common practice (sometimes more necessary than desired). Ownership entertaining itself is not the same, however. A portion of entertainment expenses may be deductible according to current IRC rules if they are considered directly related or associated with business activity.

Abuses occur when the entertainment is less related to business and more related to personal enjoyment. The deductibility of entertainment expenses is subject to strict rules.

Home Office

The most rapidly growing form of business deduction involves use of a home office. This is a result of the rapid expansion of telecommuting opportunities and the formation of home-based businesses. The Taxpayers Relief Act of 1997 (TRA 1997) provides that business deductions for home expenditures can be made if the office is used in one of the following ways:

- As a principal place of business for the business activity
- As a location to meet clients or customers during the normal course of business
- Is located in a structure not attached to the home but at the same location.

Since these tax provisions change from time-to-time, it is wise to consult current tax codes to determine actual rules covering home office use.

Deductions made are those that relate directly or indirectly to the office. This covers basic operating expenses, decorating and a prorated share of expenses that benefit the entire home. These would be mortgage interest or rent, real estate taxes, insurance, utilities and maintenance.

When a home-based business is to be acquired and moved, it is evident the home office business expenses will be discontinued. If the current owner makes deductions for the home office, they may be treated as adjustments to earnings. They will be discontinued under new ownership and cease to exist.

Interest

Mortgage interest costs are usually removed as a cost of doing business when performing an ERCON. This is because valuation formulas begin with cash flow as a key valuation variable. Committing a large portion of cash flow to the payment of a large mortgage may affect business equity. Value, however, is the combination of equity and debt. Since most valuations are performed to serve an acquisition objective, new financing is often contemplated. Therefore, interest costs related to existing financing on a business frequently changes. Existing mortgage expenses are often treated as positive adjustments to earnings.

An exception with interest can occur when financing is needed to support normal business operations. This frequently happens when inventory is financed. Interest costs related to maintenance of an inventory would not be added to earnings provided there is no change of strategy to eliminate them altogether.

Another occasion will exist when the business has wide variances in selling cycles creating the need for large cash reserves. Unless operations are funded from ownership equity (cash), interest tied to a line of credit will occur. These are not added as adjustments to earnings.

Non-recurring Expenses

There may be instances when expenses have been incurred but will not be repeated. This occurs with expenses that may be expensed rather than depreciated or amortized over time. Typical examples of non-recurring expenses are certain types of repairs and maintenance, an increase in the business inventory, addition of small equipment and so forth. If it is recognized that these costs were unique and will occur only once, they may become adjustments to earnings.

Payroll

It is common for owners of a business to pay themselves a salary. This will normally be found in the salaries or general payroll expense. It may also be placed in the officers' salaries when the business is a corporation.

In general, payroll and officers' salaries may be considered adjustments to earnings when one of the following two conditions exists.

First, payment is made from either expense to compensate a departing operating owner *who can be adequately replaced by a new operating owner*. They will acquire the existing owner's payroll and/or officer's salary.

Second are payments to compensate individuals who do not perform services for the company. Sometimes this occurs with board members or a CEO advisory board. They are compensated from officers' salaries in exchange for their participation at quarterly board meetings. If deemed unnecessary by new ownership, this expense may be treated as an adjustment to earnings.

In some cases, only a portion of the compensation to an existing owner will be recaptured as earnings. One example occurs when a new owner feels the owner's existing compensation should be split between themselves and some other type of new expense—perhaps an additional employee. Another occasion arises when a new owner elects to commit a portion of the current owner's compensation to payment of financing created to acquire the business. (This is discussed in greater detail within subsequent chapters.)

On occasion a new owner will reduce the staff of a business. This can occur if existing management has been in place for many years, has become complacent or tends to favor certain employees despite their level of performance. Eliminating jobs or people is an unpleasant as well as risky management tactic for a new owner. On the surface it does not retain the trust or loyalty of remaining employees either. Cutbacks can, however, be very timely and appropriate, plus produce a desired result: improved earnings. When this is the case, firm, decisive management is rewarded with improved earnings. This will reestablish the confidence, pride and support needed from company employees.

Conversely, no adjustment to earnings occurs when new management does not plan to replace existing management and assume their wages. This occurs occasionally when entrepreneurs target a business for addition to their portfolio and encourage existing management to continue. Or, they may hire new management altogether. Wages paid to existing management are not earnings adjustments.

Transportation

Transportation costs deducted are taxi fares, train fares, airline tickets, and so forth. These are deductible when they occur in the course of travel for business purposes. Most common of the transportation expenses is the automobile and truck expense, which frequently appears in the business operating statement. Methods of determining the auto expense taken will vary. The bigger question pertains to the use of the vehicle for business or personal purposes. Answering this question will determine the availability of adjustment if warranted.

Travel

Generally speaking, travel expenses are deductible if the owner traveled to engage in trade or business activity. Travel expenses include transportation, meals, lodging and other reasonable and necessary expenses while "away from home." The IRS takes the position that to qualify, the person traveling must be away from home overnight or for a period of time that will require some rest before returning home. Many business owners will participate in business and personal activities when traveling. The question of deductibility often occurs. The prevailing determinant is whether the travel was business or personal. There are many other rules that govern the deductibility of travel expenses that can be found in IRC rules. In any event, some travel costs appearing in business expenses may be personal or entirely unnecessary in the future. Therefore, a positive adjustment is calculated as the extent to travel costs are reduced. It is added to earnings.

The amount of adjusting estimated to occur is limited only by entrepreneurial creativity. These will always be found in the expenses of the business. Draws to ownership appearing in the balance sheet are not positive adjustments. Suspicious increases in cost of goods inferring owner's use of personal merchandise are not positive adjustments. Skimming is not. Nevertheless, when all are considered, these adjustments are capable of producing dramatic changes in the business earning power recognized. This will directly affect business value.

"Plows"
Negative Adjustments to Earnings

Negative adjustments earn the nickname "plows" because they dig into and reduce business EBIT, EBITDA and cash flow. These are expenses the business does not have prior to a transition but will incur afterward. They are not particularly common, but it is always wise to try and detect their presence.

There are many examples of negative adjustments. The most obvious is an increase in leased payments or rent occurring as a condition of a business transfer. Recent property assessments may create a rise in business or real property taxes. The husband and wife team departing as operating owners may create a need for another employee. New marketing to expand business share could be necessary. Deferred maintenance and new equipment purchases for expansion are others.

To identify negative adjustments, discuss current operations with ownership. What improvements to the business are desirable—which are required? The latter, together with any other negative adjustments, should be subtracted from cash flow.

Cash Flow Calculation

CASH FLOW CALCULATION BELL-Quest, Ltd.	
Revenue	$ 608,951
Cost of Goods	<$ 390,190 >
Gross Profit	$ 218,761
Expenses	< $189,501 >
Net Profit	$ 29,260
Interest	$ 4,533
Taxes	-----
EBIT	$ 33,793
Depreciation	$ 4,809
Amortization	$ 1,668
EBITDA	$ 40,270
Non-Recurring Expenses	$ 502
Owner's Salary	$ 18,000
CASH FLOW	$ 58,772

The completed ERCON presents a very clear estimate of the business's earning power. As previously stated, this is the business cash flow. This number may be a derivative of the most current business operating statement, or a weighted average of the past three.

One Business—Many Values

As an ERCON is performed, the buyer begins to see why a business can have many different values. Adjustments to earnings available to one investor may not be suitable for another. A situation involving any of those adjustments previously discussed could be found to apply. As a result, the cash flow available will bear a corresponding difference. The chapters describing indicators of value illustrate how cash flow affects the final result. Generally, more cash flow tends to produce a higher value estimate, and the reverse is also true.

Here, then, is a quantifiable reason one business could be worth more than one value. It depends on the needs of an interested investor. Those who can extract the most cash flow realize more benefits and can justify a larger investment.

In the end, don't try to create a one-size fits-all solution. Define, instead, a range of values. Where a business sale is anticipated, the reconstruction and value estimate should accommodate the largest target market of buyers.

CHAPTER 6

Management Compensation

What amount is the right amount?

One Hat or Two?

It is common for the same person to wear the hat of the owner and manager in a small business, receiving the dual benefits available to ownership and management. This can be a significant benefit of small business ownership. Attempting to wear both hats simultaneously, however, is a more challenging proposition. For example, both a cowboy hat and baseball cap shelter the sun from the wearer's eyes. They perform similar if not identical functions. Yet attempting to wear them both at the same time actually reduces, rather than improves, the benefit of each. They may both fit the same head—but not necessarily at the same time.

The story about hats compares to the cash flow of many small business operations that may be insufficient to pay a fair amount of management compensation plus retire debt and provide a return on equity. Nevertheless, people want to become self-employed, so buying a small business is a chance to buy a job. The danger lies in attempting to fill the roles of ownership and management simultaneously. It takes focus to execute the responsibilities of both positions efficiently. Distractions that reduce focus are the frequent results of acting both as manager and owner. This can lead to poor financial results—a primary cause of business failure.

Establishing a Pay Rate

Management compensation must be considered before it is possible to lever business cash flow into equity and debt. This is an important variable. As discussed, this should be considered separately from a return on ownership's investment, *even though the owner and manager might be the same person.* Several approaches to assign management compensation are available.

First Approach

The current ownership compensation package is always a good example to consider. Be aware, however, that many times the employment earnings of owner/operators will have become inconsistent with the local market. They own the place and can pay themselves as much or as little as they like. In some cases the salary will be small and supplemented with business profits. In others the salary is large compared to compensation for similar jobs in other businesses. It is wise to be careful when using existing management compensation (to an operating owner) as a benchmark to estimate the future cost of business supervision.

Second Approach

An alternative way to determine management compensation involves going directly to the market. Research wages other companies offer to those who would fill supervisory roles similar in skill requirements, responsibility and authority. Newspaper classified ads, industry trade journals, local accountants, lenders and competitors are good sources of accurate information. Analysts have been known to conduct surveys as a device to encourage participation and legitimate input. The results of the survey are distributed to contributors who receive the benefit of this valuable market information.

Third Approach

The U.S. Government provides a third source of data entrepreneurs can use to determine management compensation. One document available and of particular interest is the National Compensation Survey produced by the U.S. Bureau of Labor Statistics. This material describes the results of a nationwide survey of compensation amounts for hundreds of employment positions. The data shows occupation, year of survey, number of workers included in the survey and median weekly earnings for each worker. It also indicates earning variances between men and women.

INTERNET REFERENCE

Bureau of Labor Statistics
http://www.bls.gov

The Bureau of Labor Statistics is the principal fact-finding agency for the Federal Government in the broad field of labor economics and statistics. The BLS conducts a Current Population Survey (CPS) to measure the extent of unemployment in the country. The CPS has been conducted in the United States every month since 1940. Included in this report are Labor Force Statistics, including weekly earnings data.

The National Compensation Survey provides a rich source of current information for the business valuation consultant. This changes and is updated annually. To use this report correctly, identify one or more positions that match or are similar to the management position in the business under study. Working with one of these median weekly earnings values (or the average of several), multiply the weekly earnings by 52 (the number of weeks in the year) to estimate annual management costs. It is that simple; however, it is wise to challenge this estimate by comparing it to local pay levels. Thereafter, make any adjustments felt necessary in order to account for geographic or economic variances. The tables and current data on file with the United States Bureau of Labor Statistics can be found online at their website.

For the example in this text the National Compensation Survey is used. It is assumed the business is a sales-oriented enterprise.

From the job classification "Supervisors," in a Sales Occupation, the average full-time hourly wage is $19.42. The median weekly income is $776. This is $38,840 per year (50 weeks) and will be used to estimate an important business valuation variable: free cash flow.

Free Cash Flow

The rewards of ownership and employment (management) are different for everyone. By providing capital and financing, some entrepreneurs own a business without operating it. Conversely, others use their experience, skill and time to manage a business successfully but don't own it. Others find a middle ground. In all cases, all are concerned about business value. Therefore, to calculate business value it is necessary to separate the costs of management from financial rewards of ownership, as explained previously. Then business value is a derivative of earning power, assuming all the pieces and parts to deliver the return on investment are firmly in place. Leaving anything out results in an overestimation of value. The remaining funds, representing the financial reward to ownership, are free cash flow. Like its compensation counterpart, this will be used extensively in the valuation estimates.

Calculating free cash flow is easy. Cash flow is determined by performing an ERCON. When completed, the cost of management compensation is subtracted from cash flow. Free cash flow is the remainder. Examine the formula to determine this variable:

CASH FLOW CALCULATION
BELL-Quest, Ltd.

Revenue	$ 608,951
Cost of Goods	<$ 390,190 >
Gross Profit	$ 218,761
Expenses	<$ 189,501 >
Net Profit	$ 29,260
Interest	$ 4,533
Taxes	-----
EBIT	$ 33,793
Depreciation	$ 4,809
Amortization	$ 1,668
EBITDA	$ 40,270
Non-Recurring Expenses	$ 502
Owner's Salary	$ 18,000
CASH FLOW	$ 58,772
Management Compensation	<$ 38,840 >
FREE CASH FLOW	$ 19,932

Better Safe Than Sorry

As variables for valuation are developed, they become standards to define realistic investment expectations for management and ownership.

Try to remain neutral and objectively interpret data intrinsic and extrinsic [the numbers and the marketplace] to the business under review. Balance the excitement of buying or selling against marketplace variables that can be backed up (to the extent possible) with facts. A value calculated in these conditions will often meet the needs of all parties to a transaction. Buyers will not go broke attempting to make a deal that simply costs too much. Sellers will not languish in the market until it's time to give up and liquidate for half the original business value.

CHAPTER 7

Financing: Using Other People's Money

*It's the price *and* the terms.*

A business, not a home, may be the largest investment an entrepreneur will make; however, the amount of cash needed to buy a business "outright" is often more than most have available. Fortunately, it is possible to start small and grow. But financing, using other people's money, makes it possible to start a little bigger and grow a little faster. Employing this strategy over several years has great potential.

Consider the following scenario:

Growth can require cash—maybe more than business earnings produce. When this happens, it's time to find capital from other sources...other people. This is called financing, and it has an important role to help ensure that growth plans can be implemented. Without capital they often cannot. Indeed, inadequate financing is one of the key reasons most small businesses fail.

When it is time to sell out, sellers typically want as much cash as they can get. In most cases, this is possible only by working to accommodate the needs of a buyer—who may need to borrow a portion of the business purchase price.

In each instance, financing from others provides entrepreneurs with the leverage often needed to build greater wealth. Financing involves several basic elements. Learning these elements enables financing to be structured advantageously. As a consequence, the price and terms both count.

KEY INFORMATION

Suppose an entrepreneur acquires a small business worth $100,000 using a $25,000 down payment and finances the balance for five years. Business cash flows retire the debt during that time and the business appreciates at a modest rate of 1 percent annually. After the fifth year of ownership, the business is sold. Estimate 70 percent of the sales price (after taxes) is reinvested as a 25 percent down payment on another business purchased under the same conditions. This cycle is repeated four times in 20 years with the following results.

25% Initial Investment	New Business Price	Sales Proceeds Before Taxes	Cash to Pocket or Reinvest
$25,000	$100,000	$105,101	$73,571
$73,571	$294,283	$309,294	$216,506
$216,506	$866,024	$910,200	$637,140
$637,140	$2,548,559	$2,678,561	$1,874,993

From $25,000 of seed money nearly $2 million of equity is created after 20 years! This does not include compensation received and accumulated savings along the way.

Capitalization Rates

The term "capitalization rate" refers to the rate at which a stream of future payments converts into a present value. The concept is also called the "cap rate" or simply "CAP." In any case, it is expressed as a rate, like interest. For example, an investment capable of producing $1,000 of income capitalized at 10 percent indicates a present value of $10,000. As the cap rate declines, the value of the investment increases. Conversely, increasing it reduces the size of investment indicated. Consider the following examples showing the impact of a 3 percent variance in the capitalization rate.

$1,000 (income) ÷ 10% (cap) = $10,000 (value)

$1,000 (income) ÷ 8.5% (cap) = $11,764.70 (value)

$1,000 (income) ÷ 11.5% (cap) = $8,695.65 (value)

Investors who expect lower prices and greater value select higher cap rates. Buyers use higher cap rates that indicate lower investment requirements. Investors and ownership both use a capitalization rate to measure the current performance of a business. It can help set expectations of performance, such as, "The business plan for next year offers ownership a 7 percent rate of return on assets." Or it can be used to value a business when introduced with income into this indicator of value.

Notice how the capitalization formula could be used to incorporate business income (I), value (V), and a rate of return (R) expected. The latter is the capitalization rate.

Selecting a Cap Rate

There are many ways to choose a capitalization rate for investment and valuation, and it is a very important decision. The cap rate is used repeatedly to compare all business investments under consideration. Investors who focus on small publicly traded companies often establish a capitalization rate as the prime lending rate plus 12 percentage points. Using this approach with a current prime rate of 5.5 percent, the applicable capitalization rate is 17.5 percent. When the earnings per share of stock are divided by this amount, the value they will pay is indicated.

INTERNET REFERENCE

Wall Street Journal
www.wsj.com
Up-to-date information on the economy and interest rates.

Bankrate
www.bankrate.com
Helpful information on all aspects of the banking industry, including federal rates, mortgages, finance tools and calculators.

Venture capitalists invest in small businesses. They typically do not want to involve themselves with management, however, and are concerned only with ROI (return on investment). Their capitalization rate may be less, prime plus 6 percent (11.5 percent) or prime times two (11 percent), but their package of support comes with other requirements. Generally, in exchange for providing growth capital, they have options to acquire ownership for a very favorable price. Their investment horizon is five to seven years, at which time they like to sell their interest to the original ownership. The price paid will be based on the increased value of the company. In the event management is successful, the investment is lucrative. If, however, management fails to meet well-defined performance objectives, the venture capitalists can take control of the board—thus control of the company—and sell it to recover their original investment.

Angel capital investors work like venture capitalists but typically may be less aggressive. Their formulas differ to the extent that their target business investments and commitments of capital are often smaller. They frequently provide management with consulting assistance as well, which helps to ensure the company stays on track (since the original ownership is also serving as management and the potential for distractions is high). Angel capital investors expect investment terms and capitalization rates on par with their venture capital cousins.

INTERNET REFERENCE

American Bankers Association
www.aba.com
Based in Washington, D.C., the American Bankers Association represents banks of all sizes on issues of national importance for financial institutions and their customers.

Federal Deposit Insurance Corporation
www.fdic.gov
The Federal Deposit Insurance Corporation's mission is to maintain the stability of and public confidence in the nation's financial system.

Commercial banks are the most frequent users of capitalization rates. They have the closest and most frequent association with the small business sector. They invest money in these entities in the form of loans for acquisition and expansion. The interest rate charged on money loaned is the bank's return on investment.

A bank's capitalization rate is derived from its cost of money and cost of doing business. Combined, they produce what is known as the prime rate of interest—the rate charged to the bank's customers. Small business borrowers often pay the bank a few percentage points of interest over the prime lending rate, so that is the bank's capitalization rate. This can be a good benchmark for entrepreneurs to use when selecting a capitalization rate for business investing.

Capitalizing Income

Using a capitalization rate when estimating business value is helpful. This indicator of value seldom takes into consideration the differences between EBIT, EBITDA and business cash flow. In addition, they fail to account for the effects of financing on earnings. It takes money to pay off debt, and that money should come from business cash flow. Consequently, value is often indicated using the premise that debt does not exist, which is seldom true (most businesses are acquired or expanded by securing additional financing to pay the cost). The costs of servicing debt will reduce free cash flow. Actually, in some cases it will be nearly eliminated, as free cash flow is redirected from the entrepreneur to the bank. Paying off a loan instead of paying a return to investors can be a lucrative business strategy. Additional benefits can also be created by amortization of debt.

Financial Leverage

Some entrepreneurs believe nirvana is a no-money-down business acquisition. (This can be true.) Others feel the best situation is business ownership with no debt. After years of paying off a bank loan, the lure of debt-free status is very appealing. While not a mistake, a capital structure free of debt does not always maximize the earning potential of a business. Under the right conditions, financing might enhance a return on investment equity.

Leverage in business ownership is a way to acquire a business *without increasing ownership's investment* or equity. In fact, these are often reduced when investment leverage is used. Create investment leverage by borrowing more of the acquisition price. Or add debt to the capital structure of a business. Either way, less ownership equity is invested.

Can the use of financial leverage be taken too far? Absolutely! LBOs and leveraged buyouts are good examples. Investors using this strategy are so aggressive they attempt to finance entire purchase prices using no equity. This is a high-risk business strategy, because the margin for error is small.

It will be shown in future sections, describing leveraged cash flow methods of valuation, how leveraged buyouts can be structured. For the moment, remember consistent cash flows, combined with favorable earnings trends, are prerequisites to highly leveraged acquisitions. This is because servicing debt can require most, if not all, the free cash flow available. Should earnings decline, owners are faced with the unhappy proposition of supporting business debt from personal reserves.

Despite the caution, leveraging a business responsibly remains a moneymaking tool for entrepreneurs. To improve success, there are certain aspects of financing to understand and use with versatility: debt coverage ratio, loan-to-value ratio, and amortization. A discussion of each follows.

Debt Coverage Ratio

Lenders use two basic devices to limit their exposure to loss from small business loans. One limit, a debt coverage ratio, is based on business free cash flow. The second is a loan-to-value ratio based on collateral. This will be discussed later.

A debt coverage ratio (DCR) is used to discount the amount of free cash flow that can be applied to payment of debt requested. This safeguard is intended to ensure that enough cash remains available to service debt even if earnings decrease. Used in this way, the DCR is a barometer reflecting the perceived risk associated with the business cash flow of the borrower.

Usually, DCR and risk move up or down in relationship to each other. (The only exception is if DCR falls below 1.00, which, as a practical matter, does not occur.) There are few standards established for lenders to measure risk and assign a DCR. However, it is not entirely arbitrary. Borrower's credit history and proven management skills, stability of business earnings, liquidity of collateral—all are important considerations. Environmental forces can also play a role, which is particularly evident when stiff competition for the borrower's business makes an appearance. Therefore, the DCR is a subjective measurement of risk.

DCRs are generally between 1.00 and 1.50. When used to discount a cash flow, the latter is divided by the former. In the BELL-Quest, Ltd. example used throughout this text, free cash flow (FCF) is $19,932. This is money that could be treated as a return on investment for the cash investor or for payment on debt, or both. For simplicity, assume a 100 percent conversion to retire debt. Assume the lender has, based on experience, selected a debt coverage ratio of 1.10. The amount of annual debt service (ADS) that can be paid will be $18,120. This is calculated as follows:

$$\frac{\$19,932}{1.10 \ (DCR)} = \$18,120 \ (\text{Annual Debt Service})$$

Examine the table below to more fully understand the potential impact of DCR on annual debt service:

FCF	$19,932	$19,932	$19,932	$19,932	$19,932
DCR	1.00	1.20	1.30	1.40	1.50
ADS	$19,932	$16,610	$15,332	$14,237	$13,288

It is easy to see the impact of DCR. One-third of the business's free cash flow is eliminated for use as annual debt service when the debt coverage ratio is high. As a result, the amount of potential investment leverage is reduced. The DCR, then, is an important chess piece in the game of financing negotiation.

Loan-to-Value Ratios

A second device lenders use to limit exposure is a loan-to-value ratio (LTV). The loan-to-value ratio ties the amount that can be borrowed to the fair market value of assets available for collateral. For example, conventional home mortgages frequently have an LTV of 90 percent. This means the lending institution will loan the borrower up to 90 percent of the appraised value of the property. Thus, a home valued at $200,000 with a 90 percent LTV would qualify for a $180,000 mortgage.

Banks use LTVs to guard against loss of capital. If the borrower defaults on the loan, the collateral should be enough, when sold, to satisfy the remaining balance due. Take note: If the remaining loan balance is greater than the net proceeds collected from assets sold, the borrower is still responsible for paying the difference. For this reason, smart entrepreneurs attempt to negotiate "non-recourse" notes, which exempt them from such personal liability. In any event, commercial lenders know collection is an uncertain reality when a business defaults on a loan. The LTV helps prevent such losses if an entrepreneur is forced to fold.

Loan-to-value ratios are important considerations when exploring the financing option of a small business. Like their companion, DCR, they reduce the amount of leverage available to make an acquisition. It is important to be familiar with use of LTVs. They will apply to almost every business loan made by institutional lenders and denote another chess piece to move.

There are several categories of business assets that may be used as collateral for a business loan. Real estate, furnishings/fixtures/equipment, inventory and intellectual capital all have a different lifespan. Their liquidity varies, too. A bank applying a 100 percent LTV would be almost unheard of. It is more reasonable to expect LTVs for these asset classes to fall within a range roughly described as follows:

Real Estate	75% to 90%
Furnishings/Fixtures/Equipment	50% to 75%
Inventory	25% to 50%
Intellectual Capital	0% to 25%

These are estimated ranges only and may vary from lender to lender, locale to locale, and business to business. Also, keep in mind banks will seldom (if ever) offer financing using intellectual capital as collateral.

Amortization

Amortization was described earlier as an accounting charge to income based on the periodic reduction of an intangible asset's original value. A second definition is the payoff of debt through regularly timed payments of principal and interest. Payments to principal represent equal increases in equity if business value remains constant. Payments to interest are treated as deductible expenses.

Amortization of debt is useful to business indicators of value. After a DCR and LTV have been selected, it is possible to estimate the amount of debt a business can borrow. Calculating the amortization of the debt helps entrepreneurs create ways a business can afford the financing available. This will become evident in the leveraged cash flow method of valuation. Using amortization as a financing tool emphasizes the entrepreneur's ability to anticipate DCRs and LTVs, as well as calculate loan terms, interest rates, present value, future value and periodic payments on debt projected. This is the structure of financing and has a direct bearing on the benefits of financial leverage.

Using Financial Calculators

Inexpensive financial calculators help the valuation analyst work very fast. These devices have loan amortizing functions that vastly simplify the calculation of payments on debt. These instruments break the amortization calculation into five variables: term, interest, present value, future value and payment. With these calculators, it is possible to enter any four variables and easily solve for the fifth. Here are the variables involved.

1. Term - Term refers to the length of time that will pass from the origination of the loan to the payoff date. There is a general rule to follow when estimating loan terms: Don't make long-term loans on short-term assets. Otherwise, the loan will remain unpaid long after the collateral asset has experienced functional or economic obsolescence or both. The lender's risk will be unacceptable.

The term of a loan should be less than, and no more than, the useful life of the asset. Here is a general list of loan terms to use with business assets often financed, subject to regional and individual variances:

Real Estate	15 to 30 years
Furnishings/Fixtures/Equipment	3 to 7 years
Inventory	I/O - 0 to 3 Years
Intellectual Capital	N/A

I/O stands for interest only. Sometimes banks will finance an inventory using a line of credit loan. In these cases the borrower may pay interest only on the balance financed followed by periodic reductions in principal. There is no term. Since banks seldom loan on intellectual capital, no term is stated.

When entering the term of a loan into a financial calculator, it may be requested as *n*, which stands for the number of payments that will be made throughout the term. If monthly payments are called for, *n* is the term of the loan in years times twelve.

2. Interest - Interest is the cost of using money that is expressed as a rate for a period of time. The period is typically annual. As mentioned earlier, monthly payments will include interest and principal. These are calculated roughly as the interest due on the outstanding balance of the loan for the previous or coming month plus principal. The principal is the difference between the payment amount and the interest payment.

It is easy to see the interest portion of payments that occur early in the loan term will be larger than those occurring late in the loan life. This is why the same payment schedule will retire less debt early and more debt later.

KEY INFORMATION

How to Create Equity Fast!

Many investors counteract the slow reduction of loan principal with a simple technique—by making the current payment plus the small principal payment that would be due with next month's installment as they advance their amortization schedule one month. When this occurs, the interest that would have been paid is also cancelled. Executed consistently this provides a substantial savings of interest and reduces the loan term by 50 percent.

For more information about how interest rates are determined, see "Capitalization Rates" earlier in this chapter. Banks normally charge small business borrowers 1 percent to 3 percent over their prime lending rate. Interest is either fixed or variable. If fixed, it will remain constant for a specified portion (if not the entire term) of the loan. If variable, it can change periodically based on preset limits (i.e., a change of no more than 1 percent increase or decrease per period with a maximum cap of not more than 5 percent over the life of the loan). A debt with a flexible rate such as this is called an adjustable rate mortgage, or ARM.

3. Present Value - The present value of the loan is the amount borrowed. It is determined from the borrower's need or request when adjusted by the LTV, DCR, interest rate and term. A capitalization rate is used to measure the present value of a stream of payments to be collected in the future.

4. Future Value - The future value of a loan amortization is the amount of principal outstanding on the payoff date of the loan. At that time the loan balance will be zero if a loan is "fully amortized." This means the payments are enough to pay off the entire loan during the term.

In some cases, where cash flow considerations are a greater priority, equal monthly payments may not be sufficient to pay off the entire loan by the end of the loan term. An outstanding balance will be due, called a "balloon payment." In the world of finance it is common to receive a loan with an amortization term where the actual payoff of the loan from monthly payments would not occur until long after the payoff date. Loans are frequently amortized for 15 years but due in five. In this case, the term of the loan is five years.

5. Payment - The fifth variable in the amortizing equation is the amount of money needed each period to reduce the principal and pay the interest due as agreed, based on the loan term and amount. Payments may occur monthly, quarterly, semi-annually or annually. They may be amortized or include a fixed amount of principal each month plus interest on the outstanding balance.

CHAPTER 8

A Pricing Multiple for Any Business

Multiples estimate what many think they specifically measure.

Business RPM Calculator

A risk/price multiple (RPM) is often called a "pricing multiple." Multiples are popular yardsticks used to quickly indicate business value. The RPM is a subjective measure of business risk and value. Used in this way, it helps compare acquisition candidates. One can quickly measure the value from the risk indicated.

The multiple of [business] excess earnings indicator of value uses a risk/price multiple. It can also function as a guide to management since it will illustrate a business's weaknesses and strengths. It also can be used to help determine management compensation bonuses.

Risk/price multiples are more commonly used, however, as quick estimates of business value, because they are so simple. For example, a business with a higher multiple is perceived as a better business than one with a lower multiple. This means the risk is less, so the value is more.

The risk/price multiple appears in many valuation rules of thumb, too. These are stated as "five times earnings" or "one times revenue" in many service businesses. Formulas using an RPM can be quick and helpful indicators of value if developed from sound premises. Unfortunately this is not always the case.

KEY INFORMATION

Sounds Good—But Is It Really?

Consider a most common multiple: "five times earnings." Business owners ready to sell out often dream of notoriously high multiples. Values indicated may not offer investors enough cash flow to compensate management, provide a return on investment or service acquisition debt. The price indicated can be so high that it is laughable. Buyers work in reverse—they prefer a multiple so low it would be possible to finance 150 percent of an acquisition price from free cash flow. The business is probably worth more than their highly leveraged estimate of value.

To further confuse the use of multiples, no clear definition is often given to the type of earnings used with the multiple. Is it net profit, EBIT, EBITDA, cash flow or free cash flow? Clearly, net profit and free cash flow will produce very different values using the same RPM. One must also question selection of the variable "5." Is it a function of the owners' desire to sell for more than the business is worth or more than what might be indicated by comparable sales? The last option sounds most credible, but only if RPMs used are developed from an accurate set of "comps." There is a better way.

Work from the Inside *and* Outside

Consider building an RPM using intrinsic business elements in addition to these other methods. Comparative data, seller expectations and buyer demands are balanced with business indicators of performance as predictors of value. These may limit the RPM's ability to produce a reliable result. Developing a risk/price multiple from external *and internal* characteristics is a better way. It takes more time and investigation, but the tool created is useful and meaningful enough to more than justify the effort.

Many Kinds of Risk to Measure

Risk in business is the possibility of losing value or failing to increase value. There are many kinds of risk: appreciation risk, inflation risk, interest rate risk, inventory risk, liquidity risk, political risk, repayment risk and risk to principal.

While all types of risk are important to small business entrepreneurs, appreciation, liquidity, inventory, repayment and risk to principal are of greatest concern.

Appreciation risk pertains to the ability of the business to grow in value. There are many reasons this can occur. Some are beyond the control of ownership; others are not. Recall, amortization applies responsible financial leverage to produce a gradual increase in ownership equity. This occurs as debt is reduced, although the potential gain available, though desirable, remains finite. Appreciation, on the other hand, offers infinite potential for increases in business value. Effective management of financial leverage, combined with gradual appreciation, has the potential to create impressive wealth over time. It also reduces the risk to principal.

Liquidity risk is created by the possibility the business will run out of cash. The reason is, quite simply, when a business is out of cash, it is out of options. When options to carry on are removed, the business can easily fail.

Inventory risk is capturing increased attention. Dell Computer enjoys a commanding lead in the computer manufacturing industry due, in part, to their successful system of inventory management. With sales of millions per day, they have only a short-term supply of inventory on hand. Dramatic levels of functional and economic obsolescence constantly occurring in the hardware industry create great risk. Millions of dollars invested in stagnant inventory does not enhance business performance. Dell's unique approach to inventory management reduces this risk considerably.

Objectivity Would Be Nice …

Unfortunately, there are so many different types and sizes of small businesses that a one-size-fits-all business multiple, even for specific industries, is hard to develop. That is the state of the small business environment. Multiples do remain helpful, though, and can be created from objective information.

As indicated, several factors affect development of a useful risk/price multiple. It is not possible to produce a perfect indicator of performance. The process is subjective: It's determined by the perceptions of the person conducting the analysis. With good material from a complete due diligence, the analyst can develop an RPM that is highly defensible.

To calculate a risk/price multiple, the following approach is recommended. Separate the business into six or seven categories: finance, control, marketing, sales, production, service and intellectual capital (the latter is an optional category). Notice they correspond to those recommended in a due diligence investigation.

Each category is assigned a value from 0 to 5. Category values are the average of five subcategories representing characteristics of that category. These subcategories also receive a value from 0 to 5. With both categories and subcategories, high numbers indicate better quality and less risk, whereas lower numbers mean low quality and greater risk. When selecting values for each category or subcategory, it may be helpful to use the following scale for easy reference:

SCALE OF VALUES
TO MEASURE BUSINESS RPM

0	MAXIMUM RISK – "Radioactive!"	Business out of control. Failure is likely.
1	HIGH RISK – "Not with my money you don't."	Loss of equity likely. Crisis management prevails.
2	RISKY – "This is going to be a problem."	Small margins for error, but recovery is possible.
3	ACCEPTABLE RISK – "A test of patience and will."	Market and management forces can prevail.
4	LOW RISK – "Bet half the savings."	Good control over growth and equity. Secure.
5	MINIMAL RISK – "Money in the bank!"	Excellent control, many opportunities, and profitable.

The category values are averaged, and the result is the business risk/price multiple—its RPM—and an indicator of value derived from factors internal and forces external to the business.

The long-form RPM calculator can be found in Appendix C. Here is the short form:

BUSINESS RPM
BELL-Quest, Ltd.

1	Finance	3.0
2	Control	3.0
3	Marketing	1.0
4	Sales	2.0
5	Production	4.0
6	Service	4.0
7	Intellectual Capital	1.0
	Total	18.0
	Variables	÷7
	Business RPM	2.57

Putting It All Together

The subcategories suggested for use in calculating a business RPM may vary. Investor interests, business types and market conditions can cause this to occur. Flexibility is important, too. Entrepreneurs building risk/price multiples may elect to make substitutions to better suit their needs.

In addition, the work to create a business RPM can become as detailed as one chooses to make it. Clearly, to develop precise information about each subcategory might require extensive investigation. Values assigned, however, remain a subjective interpretation of the entrepreneur or valuation analyst. So while investigation is a healthy exercise, one can reach a point of diminishing return.

By all means, perform a complete due diligence. Or make the due diligence as complete as time and resources permit. Then step away, adopt a fresh perspective and quickly evaluate or score each subcategory. Recalculate the business RPM. As before, first impressions based on good data most often prove correct.

Suggested RPM Categories and Subcategories

Here, together with thoughts to consider and questions to ask, are the categories and subcategories used to develop the risk/price multiple.

Finance

Trailing revenue - Emphasis is on historical trends. Is revenue increasing each year, holding steady or declining? Normally, steadily increasing revenues are signs of a well-run business. In this case, risk would be low, so the value selected would be greater. Risk is low, so the multiple is high.

Declining revenue is usually an indication of lower demand for business goods and services. That could be related to poor quality or limited production capability affecting product availability. This deserves careful study; however, declining revenue is always a strong indicator of greater business risk. Do not automatically consider rapid increases in revenue as favorable developments. Growth is the hardest part of a business to manage. Growth requires increases in capital spending to support production. If demand suddenly stops after significant investments in infrastructure have been made, cash reserves may run dry. Risk is increased.

Revenue momentum - Significant annual improvements in business revenue are generally extrapolated into continuing increases called momentum. Determining how much momentum, translated as increased revenue, will occur next year and the year after is more difficult. This involves forecasting, which is challenging and uncertain. Unlike risk, uncertainty cannot be adequately measured.

History remains the best predictor of the future. Provided the forces that feed increases in trailing revenues remain viable, one might extrapolate continuing changes of the same, greater or lesser degree. Companies with higher momentum supported by premises expected to remain in place have less risk and a higher value.

83

Companies with no momentum or reverse momentum have a high risk and are assigned a low value.

Capital structure - How financially fit is the business? To determine a value for this subcategory, examine business debt and equity. When debt is more than double equity (using market value of assets), the business is highly leveraged. Risk is greater. Conversely, a business with no debt may not be risk free. It may have a lower ROI. A capital structure can also be a sign of management complacency. The business could be missing marketing opportunities repeatedly. If the business is not keeping pace, a growth wall may have been built or may be under construction. The business may not be able to handle debt. Risk could be greater. Look closely.

Leverage opportunities - Remember, one tactic to increase return occurs with financial leverage. Businesses with no debt, as just described, may not enjoy the opportunity to create financial leverage. Since risk is greater, return is lower. More importantly, financial leverage may be required to keep pace with the market. If it is not affordable, risk is greater. Businesses that can employ financial leverage to improve ROI, or to stay ahead of competitors, enjoy less risk and a higher value.

Earnings and cash flow - Clearly, those businesses with cash flow sufficient to accomplish ownership objectives are most desirable. The presence of cash increases access to more strategies. More available strategies extend the life and profitability of a business. It can be a tougher competitor. Ample cash flows reduce risk; limited cash flow increases risk.

Control

Employee turnover rates and costs - The inability to hire and retain quality employees can put a company out of business. The rate of turnover among employees is a reflection of job fit. One wrests control of business functions from management by forcing a focus on replacing and retraining people. The other seizes control of business earnings. This is a crucial consideration in a tight labor market, which many experts say will continue for the next 10 to 15 years.

Employee turnover rates are calculated as the number of employees leaving each year, for whatever reason, as a percentage of the total people employed. The national average is high, approximately 16 percent, which means 16 percent of the people that are employed today will be gone one year from today. Most companies discover their rate is as high as 30 percent. Turnover reduces management control.

Employee turnover costs are also much higher than most expect. It is not uncommon for the indirect and direct costs of employee turnover to exceed an employee's annual salary.

Both employee turnover rates and costs are a threat to management's control. Examine how the business addresses the issue of job fit and environment to encourage longevity. Aggressive measures reduce risk. If no measures are in place to deal with this hidden menace, risk is greater.

Employee compensation - Nothing motivates people like having a piece of the pie. Nothing demoralizes employees faster than being treated unfairly. To resolve both, management may install a written, company-wide compensation policy. With a policy in writing, trust is improved and people will perceive management as more fair. When incentives to perform behaviors that lead to improved financial results are in place, people are rewarded with validation and money. If these are delivered in amounts that are comparable with alternative employment, the system will be productive. Risk is less.

Contingency planning - Does the business have a financial plan with a revenue and expense forecast? If so, risk is a little less. Does the business have a Plan "B" or "C" in the event Plan "A" fails to produce? It is certain that at least part of the original plan won't work. Options reduce risk.

Another factor affecting control and contingency planning is management's flow of control. Ownership that supports management by committee or chain of command will be outmaneuvered and outrun by aggressive competitors. Reactions are slow and often occur when it is too late. Risk is greater.

Absence of a reaction plan also increases risk. Because business moves so fast, companies must be in position to react swiftly. Unpredictable changes occur almost daily. How well does the company react to constant unpredictability? In the fast-paced world of e-commerce, a good reaction plan may be the best way to reduce risk to control. Risk would be less. In the absence of a reaction, strategic operating or financial plan, risk is higher.

Network penetration - A company that builds a product that can be used by only one person is not penetrating the network of consumers available. A company that builds a product that can be used by more than one person does a better job. A company that builds a product, such as meaningful information sent by e-mail that can be read by one million people, enjoys exciting network penetration. With greater network penetration, risk is less. With no network penetration, how can the business keep pace with businesses that have developed this resource?

Potential litigation - Every business can be subject to claims from customers and competitors. Does the business have a history of lawsuits? Is there any pending litigation? Are there any outstanding judgments? One measure of exposure to litigation is activity that draws fire. Another measure is how well a company builds a defensive shield to prevent the impact of litigation should it occur. When the record shows a history of lawsuits, the risk is high. Where there are none, and counter-measures are in place, risk is less.

Marketing

Well-defined marketing plan - Does the company have a written marketing plan? The ability to follow the plan to identify core values of the company with those of its target market is the key link to sales. With no plan to define and execute marketing, risk is very high. With a well-executed plan, risk is reduced.

Branded power - A brand exists to create trust. To do that it must be memorable and recognizable. It has to be delivered frequently and consistently to produce results. On the Internet, a company's brand is its substitute for the bricks and mortar of a business.

Companies that successfully brand themselves will have less risk in the future compared to those that don't.

Market differentiation - Risk to a business will increase if it cannot differentiate itself from competitors. A business must be able to tell customers why it is different and why it is better. If it cannot, there is no reason for customers to patronize one business over another. When differentiation is effective, however, risk can be reduced.

Market segmentation - One does not need to sell his or her products and services to everyone in the world to be successful – just to everyone with a need for what is offered.

KEY INFORMATION

Kellogg's *Grape Nuts* is a breakfast cereal that sells to just 2 percent of the total breakfast cereal market. That small share of the market is worth $160 million a year. Because of this effective market segmentation, *Grape Nuts* is a 100-year-old company (that doesn't even sell grapes or nuts). Companies that do not know who their target market or market segment is—and therefore fail to attract them—have greater risk.

E-commerce activity - Companies that have no plan to participate in e-commerce activity have the greatest risk. It doesn't matter if they can't deliver a hamburger in cyberspace—they can use the medium to attract customers. It is said that companies with no e-commerce function will become extinct, and soon. "To attract more customers—become more attractive."

Sales

Type of service/product - Understanding the physical characteristics of a product or service is not enough to eliminate risk. One must understand what is offered in terms of its transactional, consultative or enterprise characteristics. One is a soft drink, another is advice and the third is a partnership. Failure to recognize these differences, and how they are changing, creates greater risk.

Sales process fit - Among the most common mistakes made in sales is the mismatch of sales technique, or process, to product type. The sales process must improve the value of the product. Otherwise, it should be eliminated entirely so the product can enjoy greater price/competitive advantages and greater sales. When a mismatch occurs, the cost of sales is too high in relation to the results received. Risk is higher.

Sales incentives available - Ross Perot is a billionaire. So was Ewing Kauffman, founder of Marion Labs. Both were salespeople whose management limited their earning capability. Both quit their jobs and started their own companies for the wide-open territory of entrepreneurship. Are the business's salespeople given incentives that treat them like employees or like entrepreneurs? The latter reduces business risk.

Sales training programs - As with advertising, when business becomes unfavorable, the training budget is often cut first. This does not lead to improved results. The existence of training programs in a company reduces risk. The use of them at the right time reduces it more.

Wired distribution - The no-brainer of the 21st century is distributing services via the Internet. The gains one can make in time, flexibility and costs are worth more over the long term than the development costs. As previously stated, a close association with Internet commerce reduces risk.

Production

Emphasize quality - In the absence of quality, errors will increase. This is not a new concept. William Edwards Demming introduced it as the Demming Management Method. The premise of this method is simple: More errors result in greater production costs and lower earnings. That increases risk. What steps are taken in the flow of production and service to ensure that quality stays high? "Quality costs when you don't have it."

Innovation - In business one is either moving forward or backward. This is because standing still permits a business to fall behind compared to others sustaining forward motion. Which direction a business moves has its genesis in the business's innovative spirit. Even the Industrial Age suggestion box is an attempt to find new ideas. Employees, who see all the problems in a business first hand, have the innovative solutions needed to remove them. In the fast-paced world of business today, how well management draws out this innovative element will affect business risk favorably or unfavorably.

Capacity vs. demand - If business has the ability to produce more than it delivers, risk to revenue is less, provided there is a growing demand for products and services produced. Companies without the capacity to meet demand are growing, but also have greater risk to their survival.

Obsolescence - Whether functional or economic, obsolescence has been shown to be a loss of asset value. Risk to principal increases in the face of obsolescence. Examine production process and equipment for obsolescence. It is a direct measure of business risk.

Inventory management - It was mentioned previously that Dell Computer Company has used sound principles of inventory management to reduce risk. Another device is access to inventory. Examine how well the business maximizes its ability to order, receive and manage inventory. Those who do it most efficiently, for the least amount of investment, have the least risk.

Service

Customer satisfaction - This is an intangible asset that money cannot buy. Good impressions on the part of customers are hard to earn. They are easy to keep as long as service is maintained. If lost, satisfaction takes years to rebuild. The analyst should take the time to interview a few customers of the business and attempt to determine their level of satisfaction. If the business is well thought of, risk is less.

Employee recognition - Pay is not a motivator. Recognition from a peer group is more powerful. Businesses that recognize this important concept offer programs that recognize superior achievement. Employees respond with superior performance. When employees are recognized for their hard work the risk is less.

Team spirit - Peter Drucker has said a management team is one of the most powerful new tools in the manager's toolbox. Teams assigned to specific functions have the potential to produce more results, as a unit, than the team members functioning individually. Teams help businesses reduce risk.

Flexibility - Stellar service in small businesses is often linked to flexibility. It can be their greatest strength when facing larger competitors that are often unable to quickly adapt to marketplace changes. As a result, growth walls are less likely to develop in a small entrepreneurial company. Their search for new ideas is constant. When found, they are quickly put to use. Flexibility and adaptability reduce risk.

Open communication - Employees, customers and associates represent a rich source of feedback. This information has the potential to offer the most valuable service improvements a company can achieve. Companies that encourage communication from all sources have less chance of losing touch with the marketplace—and less risk.

Intellectual Capital

Vision - The old adage still applies: "It is easier to cross the country with a map and a destination than by wandering aimlessly about." Without a vision of where the business is headed, uncertainty can prevail in the minds of customers, employees, investors and professional representatives. Being a winner means knowing what winning means. Everyone wants to hitch his or her wagon to a winner.

Integrated vision - Look for signs the vision is integrated into the everyday thinking of employees and customers. This improves retention and results. It is the foundation of quality service. With no vision, crisis management can prevail and risk is higher.

Employee autonomy - Are employees given an environment where they can do whatever is necessary to produce results? Is this type of autonomy encouraged? These forces, combined with others, build employee motivation. Try to imagine a business succeeding when the employees don't care. The risk will be very high.

Synergy This occurs when combined expenses produce a result that is greater than the two expenses treated separately. Synergy is the basis for many business mergers. Operating costs for the new entity are lower while revenues and earnings increase. Synergies are easy to find but hard to make work, however. In fact, many companies that grow by acquisition discover in the final analysis that the cost did not outweigh the benefits. Still, the presence of synergy among categories considered in the risk/price multiple can reduce risk.

Key people - Management and people are important assets in a business. Unfortunately, some expect to be treated in a manner that is disproportionate to their value. Look for redundancy in job functions; does more than one person know how to perform a critical skill? Where this exists, risk resulting from the loss of a key employee is less.

Institutional intelligence - Coca-Cola has a secret formula. Microsoft has a source code. None can argue that the value of this institutional intelligence has propelled both to roles as corporate leaders on a global scale. Institutional intelligence is an old idea that continues to thrive in a new economy. As with people, businesses can have trade secrets that represent a rich source of intellectual capital. These are patents, copyrights, production processes or consumer intelligence. When properly leveraged these intangible assets can provide a distinctive competitive edge. That reduces risk. When all competitors are able to do the same thing, risk is greater.

CHAPTER 9

Indicator of Value I: Capitalizing Income

"I could have used one of many equations to calculate the theory of relativity. I chose the simple one."
—Paraphrased from Albert Einstein

Capitalizing business income represents a "market" approach to estimating business value. This is because it relies on comparable [capitalization] rates of return that might be available from other business opportunities. Therefore, selecting the best capitalization rate and most appropriate form of business income are important considerations when using this technique. They will affect the valuation estimate.

In Essence

A very simple equation is used to calculate this indicator of value. It is surprisingly easy to do. All one needs to do is select the proper variables and apply basic multiplication and division skills. A common name for the equation used to execute the capitalization method is the IRV formula. It is given this name because the equation uses three variables, which are I (income), R (rate or cap rate) and V (value). Using the business earning power (intrinsic qualities) and rates of return investors expect (extrinsic qualities), the valuation consultant can easily calculate a business value. The IRV equation is:

$$\frac{I}{R \times V}$$

By using any two of these variables, it is possible to calculate the third.

$$Income = Rate \times Value$$

$$Rate = \frac{Income}{Value}$$

$$Value = \frac{Income}{Rate}$$

Therefore, when one knows the income produced by an investment, and the market rate expected, it is possible to quickly estimate the cash value of the investment. Alternatively, one who knows the rate of return expected and the value, or asking price, can estimate the income that should be available from that business. And knowing the income produced and the business value enables the valuation consultant to calculate the capitalization rate of return available.

KEY INFORMATION

It Pays to Be Flexible.

This indicator of value can be used to quickly pre-qualify business investments. An investor seeking to acquire a business will know the asking price and acceptable cap rates. Multiplying one by the other suggests the amount of income that should be available. A simple earnings reconstruction can be performed to determine if this is the case. If the actual income is less than estimated, the business may be overpriced. If the income is more than estimated, the business could represent a good value.

It is possible to calculate this indicator of value from income, too. Divide it by the asking price to estimate the rate of return. Or divide it by the cap rate to produce the indicator of value.

Use the Correct Variables

Remember, effective results depend on selecting good variables. Capitalizing income is no exception. Follow these steps to produce the best results when using the formula.

STEP 1: Select the Correct Income

Four types of income can be used when capitalizing business income: EBIT, EBITDA, cash flow, and free cash flow. In most cases free cash flow—cash flow less estimated management compensation—is the best choice. Review the earnings summary from the example presented earlier.

STEP 2: Select the Right Rate of Return (Cap Rate)

The earlier discussion of cap rates used in small business valuation indicated several approaches are available to set the rate. There also are several rates to consider. Interest rates can vary widely over time. To account for these variances and maintain a consistent approach throughout this text the following rates are used but can be expected to change over time.

Federal lending rate	2.5%
Prime lending rate (P)	5.5%
Small business lending rate	P to P+<2.00% 5.5% to 7.5%
SBA lending rate	P to P+2.25-2.75% 5.5% to 8.25%
Safe rate (Corporates & Municipals)	4.5% to 5.5%

From these benchmarks one might develop an "opportunity" rate that would be synonymous with the capitalization rate. A good starting point is prime times two [5.5% x 2 = 11%].

STEP 3: Calculate the Value

Divide the income by the rate. This is the value of the investment indicated. Assume maximum SBA lending rates as applicable investor's capitalization rate.

$$\$19,932 \text{ (I)} \div 11.0\% \text{ (R)} = 181,200 \text{ (V)}$$

Capitalizing this income indicates a business value of $181,200. This value, taken from trailing earnings, will provide an investor with an 11 percent return on investment after costs of compensation to management. Entrepreneurs who prefer to operate their business investments would receive management earnings in addition to their return. The combined financial benefit to an operating owner is $58,772. This is how many small business owners perceive and measure the economic reward available to ownership.

The formula for capitalizing business income looks like this.

$$\frac{\text{Income @ \$19,932}}{\text{Rate @ 11.0\%}} = \text{Value @ \$181,200}$$

As mentioned, the income of an investment is frequently unavailable in the early stages of an entrepreneur's discovery process. Following is an illustration of how using the equation with different variables can produce an alternative value. At a given value of $181,200 and investor expected ROI of 11.0 percent, income should be:

$$11.0\% \ (R) \times \$181,200 \ (V) = \$19,932 \ (I)$$

Substituting Variables

Suppose free cash flow is less. How will this affect the business value and rate of return? Using business income of $15,000 with no change in the asking price indicates the rate of return will be 8.28 percent.

$$\$15,000 \ (I) \div \$181,200 \ (V) = 8.28\% \ (R)$$

The investor has a decision to make. Is the ROI of 8.28 percent still acceptable, despite its variance from the market rate preferred? Or, can the value be adjusted so the desired rate of return is preserved? To calculate the value indicated by the lower income:

$$\$15,000 \text{ (I)} \div 11.0\% \text{ (R)} = \$136,364 \text{ (V)}$$

The new value indicated is considerably less.

IF CASH FLOW IS HIGHER than suggested, adjusting the formula increases the rate available. To compensate, ownership may elect to raise the value.

$$\$25,000 \text{ (I)} \div \$181,200 \text{ (V)} = 13.8\% \text{ (R)}$$

Or

$$\$25,000 \text{ (I)} \div 11.0\% \text{ (R)} = \$227,273 \text{ (V)}$$

Capitalize income to quickly indicate business value. The flexibility of variable substitution permits easy calculation of alternative results compared to benchmarks and other investments. Verify the results with valuation techniques derived from cost and income indicators that follow.

CHAPTER 10

Indicator of Value 2: Multiple of Excess Earnings

What is goodwill worth?

A second indicator of value that is easy to learn and use is the multiple of excess earnings. It is similar to a real estate cost approach because costs to acquire tangible and intangible property are added to indicate value. This technique helps define what these are worth if purchased separately or if alternative businesses capable of producing the same economic result were acquired instead. A correlation to asset values differentiates the multiple of excess earnings technique from other indicators of value.

Excess Earnings

Excess earnings are business free cash flow less a return on the market value, or cost, of tangible business assets. The resulting amount is inferred to be cash generated by the business goodwill or "intangibles."

This indicator of value is widely used. Although it works well with businesses that are asset intensive, it can also prove useful with service companies where dependence on unique people or assets is high. Obviously, it's a good approach for small businesses because it quickly separates the value of hard assets from "goodwill." The value of the latter is a pressing concern for most business owners and investors.

🔑 KEY INFORMATION

"What's my goodwill worth?"

This is a question business owners often ask during their term of ownership. Their calculation of goodwill is often a groundless estimate plucked out of thin air with no basis in logic. Here is a response to offer regardless of the owner's estimate. "First, goodwill is only one type of a class of property known as intangible assets. Their value is calculated after business value is determined. The value of intangibles, including goodwill, is the difference between a business's overall value and the fair market value of its tangible assets." This leads the business owner directly into a discussion of the benefits and procedures to determine business value. This is the objective.

This indicator of value helps confirm or improve on value estimated by capitalizing business income.

To calculate a multiple of excess earnings, the following variables are needed:

- Free cash flow
- Market value of tangible assets
- Safe rate of return
- Business RPM

Free cash flow, market value of tangible assets and RPM are developed as described earlier. A safe rate of return is the return on investment or "interest rate" one might receive from a highly liquid short-term investment such as a high-quality corporate or municipal bond.

With these variables in place, value may be estimated using the following steps.

STEP 1: Determine Business Free Cash Flow

This figure comes from the ERCON prepared to identify cash flow adjusted for management compensation.

Business Free Cash Flow = $19,932

STEP 2: Calculate a Return on Tangible Assets

Ask, "What could the investment in market value of tangible assets be earning if the money were invested elsewhere?" To determine this, multiply their market value by the safe rate of return.

The market (not book) value of assets includes (for purposes of a business sale), the following assets:

- Real Estate @ $105,000

- Inventory @ cost totaling $55,000

- Furnishings, Fixtures and Equipment @ $5,000

- Total $165,000

$$
\begin{array}{rl}
\$\ 165,000 & \\
\text{X} \quad\quad 4.5\% & \text{(safe rate of return)} \\
\hline
\$\quad 7,425 & \text{(return on tangible assets)}
\end{array}
$$

STEP 3: Determine the Business Excess Earnings

Subtract the return on investment in tangible assets (see Step 2) from free cash flow.

	$19,932	(free cash flow)
less	$ 7,425	(return on tangibles)
	$12,507	(excess earnings)

STEP 4: Calculate Market Value of Business Excess Earnings

This is the excess earnings multiplied by the business RPM.

	$12,507	(excess earnings)
X	2.57	(RPM)
	$32,143	(excess earnings or goodwill)

STEP 5: Determine Estimated Business Value

Add the market value of business excess earnings to the market value of business tangible assets.

	$165,000	(tangibles)
+	$ 32,143	(value of excess earnings)
	$197,143	(business value)

Applying the Multiple of Excess Earnings Technique

Use the excess earnings method to complement or confirm value determined by capitalizing income. As mentioned, this technique makes it easy to identify how much goodwill is worth. Notice how the formula automatically assigns a value to goodwill by identifying the income it creates. With this ability, it's easy to measure the growth of goodwill by recalculating value over time.

 KEY INFORMATION

"Don't try to eat a plateful of potential!"

Many buyers have discovered that business sellers often attempt to justify value by emphasizing how much more their business could be worth if certain initiatives were taken. A smart buyer will request predictions of investment required and income produced. Thereafter, the multiple of excess earnings can be used to predict changes in tangible asset values and free cash flow and, from there, the "potential" business value is calculated. One quickly discovers that the effort to create additional goodwill may not be as productive as envisioned. This is a good tool and technique for buyers dealing with sellers attempting to sell business potential instead of current or trailing earnings.

MULTIPLE OF EXCESS EARNINGS
BELL-Quest, Ltd.

VARIABLES:

Free Cash Flow		$ 19,932
Safe Rate		4.5%
Tangible Assets		$165,000
RPM		2.57
Business Free Cash Flow		$ 19,932
Tangible Assets	165,000	
Safe Rate of Return	4.50%	
Return on Tangible Assets		<7,425>
Business Excess Earnings		$ 12,507
Risk/Price Multiple		2.57
Value of Excess Earnings		$ 32,143
Value of Tangible Assets		$165,000
MULTIPLE OF BUSINESS EXCESS EARNINGS		$197,143

Like capitalizing income, a multiple of excess earnings is easy to do and produces a logical, meaningful result if the variables selected are accurate.

CHAPTER 11

Indicator of Value 3: Levering Cash Flow

Make cash work more, so you work less.

What Buyers Want

Levering cash flow into a return on equity and retirement of debt is a powerful indicator of business value. It addresses three important buyer concerns: 1) provide for management compensation; 2) pay a return on equity; and 3) retire debt created to acquire the business. The value indicated includes an estimate of all three based on initial assumptions that ultimately define a transaction structure. This immensely practical approach is the gold standard of indicators of business value. It's what you can afford to pay.

Those interested in buying a business are really replacing a job someone else owns with a job of their own. That's not a glamorous perspective, but it is realistic. As such, emphasis is often on replacing employment and paying off business debt. In most cases a return on equity would be a bonus. Also, most small businesses that sell often involve some type of acquisition financing. Leverage is attractive to buyers seeking to maximize the value of their equity or down payment. Owners sensitive to a buyer's needs price their businesses with this method and sell them faster.

Levering cash flow is an acid test to challenge overpriced business opportunities. If the price doesn't make sense, adjust the calculation to identify a more acceptable result. Owners, uncertain about how value is calculated, often overprice them to "play it safe." Bad strategy.

Levering cash flow is flexible and versatile, too. Variables are easily changed to examine different options. These may vary from market to market or business type to business type. This flexibility is needed when valuing small businesses because no two are alike.

EFFECTIVE PHRASE

"Will the cash flow pay me a salary, a return on my equity and retire the financing?"

Easy question to ask. Tough to answer because it's a direct challenge to value. Use it early and save a lot of time and effort. Most owners won't have a well-prepared response, because there's not enough cash flow. This is what happens when a business is overpriced, and it is an opportunity to take control. Use this technique to indicate the business value and justify a different position…yours. You will learn if the seller is motivated to sell or just playing games.

Leverage Built-In

That's what management compensation, a return on equity, and financing are when this indicator of value is calculated. Free cash flow is used to pay a return on equity and retire debt that is routinely secured. There are two primary sources of financing. One, a bank, will offer more restrictive terms than the other, a seller. Variations in financing terms will affect the cost or amount of financing available. This in turn affects the price in such a way that one type of financing typically produces a lower value than the other. Therefore, the cash flow method of valuation is presented in two forms: one with seller financing and the other with financing from a commercial lender. Together they help build a value range based on business performance. Comparing values derived from the leveraged cash flow methods (with capitalized income and a multiple of excess earnings estimates of value) expands and improves the range of values.

Seller Financing

Business owners want to sell out for the highest price, in the shortest time, for the least effort. Financing the sale to a buyer is a good way to accomplish this objective. There are other reasons owners finance businesses they sell. Financing from a bank is harder to secure; it takes longer, more disclosures are required, it's more expensive, and it drives the business value down. By comparison, seller financing is a path of least resistance and it will make the opportunity more attractive. Compared to banks, sellers also have more faith in, and a willingness to accept, tangible and intangible assets as collateral for debt. They have direct experience with the ability of these assets to produce a financial result. Seller financing provides regular monthly income, perhaps for retirement, following years of building a business. Also, the terms can work to the advantage of a seller. The business value might be higher. Here are factors to consider when contemplating seller financing.

Interest Rates and Terms

Interest rates for sellers who finance their property can often be the same as those charged by a local lender. This is normally acceptable to buyers unless interest rates start to rise so high that the cost of financing dramatically affects the price. Just such a situation occurred in the late 1970s and early 1980s when interest rates were as high as 20 percent. Business sellers took advantage of this opportunity by offering buyers a much more desirable, lower rate.

INTERNET REFERENCE

http://www.federalreserve.gov

The Federal Reserve, the central bank of the United States, was founded by Congress in 1913 to provide the nation with a safer, more flexible, and more stable monetary and financial system.

Today the Federal Reserve's duties fall into four general areas: (1) conducting the nation's monetary policy; (2) supervising and regulating banking institutions and protecting the credit rights of consumers; (3) maintaining the stability of the financial system; and (4) providing certain financial services to the U.S. government, the public, financial institutions, and foreign official institutions.

Sometimes a seller will attempt to boost the sale price with substantial reductions in the interest rate charged on financing. IRS regulations set a floor on the interest rate charged in an installment sale. In these instances the IRS will treat the transaction as if a base rate of interest were charged that is greater than unstated interest collected. The effect of this treatment is a conversion of gross profit (from the sale of a business) that might have been more preferentially treated as a capital gain into ordinary income. The taxes due will be greater. These rules are complex, however, and as with all other references to Tax Code Provisions, seek advice from a qualified tax consultant.

The second financing variable to consider is the term. A general rule to help determine this variable is: "The life of the loan should be equal to, or less than, the service life of the asset securing the debt." Using this premise, a ten-year loan on an investment of videotapes for a video rental store might be inappropriate. Conversely, a three-year term for land with a new building is not long enough.

Businesses without real estate and including only personal property (furnishings, fixtures, equipment and inventory) are often financed for three, five or seven years. The difference is based on the business RPM, trailing and current earnings, cash flows, LTV, DCR and qualifications of the buyer.

Where real estate is used to secure the loan, in addition to business personal property, the financing term is normally 15 years, but it can be more. Also, separate loans may be made for the real estate and one or more categories of personal property.

Like its companion variable, interest rate, the longer the term, the more financing available. Yet, one would not expect a seller to be positioned holding a 30-year loan on business real estate where obsolescence can easily occur. Most common are 15-year terms or the alternative of a 20-year amortization with a 15-year due date. Be conservative.

Determining Equity Set-Aside

To identify buyer's equity, work in reverse. First, estimate the buyer's equity as a percent of the total indicated business value. In other words, what percent of down payment would the buyer be expected to contribute...25 percent, 33 percent, 50 percent?

Next, using percent of buyer's equity set-aside from the free cash flow funds that will be used to provide a return on equity; e.g., 25 percent equity related to a 25 percent equity set-aside from the free cash flow. This will be capitalized at the capitalization rate selected earlier for use in the capitalization of income indicator of value to produce an estimate of buyer's equity.

For example, assume a business has $40,000 of free cash flow and buyer's equity is estimated at 25 percent [of the acquisition price] with a capitalization rate of 11 percent. The equity set-aside would be $10,000 ($40,000 x 25%) and buyer's equity would be $90,909 ($10,000/11%). This is the amount that will be added to financing to indicate the business value.

The Financing Involved

Four steps are needed to use levering cash flow indicator of business value. To begin, retrieve free cash flow available from the ER-CON performed in a due diligence. Be sure to use trailing earnings from the most current business fiscal year. If trends are strong, use a weighted value taken from two or three years past. Avoid using projected earnings since too many things can cause them to change. Also, the free cash selected will presume that an appropriate value for management compensation is considered.

Next, divide annual debt service into a stream of monthly payments. These will service the debt created. Divide the annual free cash flow by 12, since monthly payments are normally requested.

Third, determine the amount of debt the annual and monthly debt service can support. (Recall the discussion of amortization as it pertains to financing.) The payment is identified in step two above. Next, select a loan term, interest rate and future value at the due date of the loan (usually zero). From these variables the loan amount is calculated.

Last, add equity [capitalized from the equity set-aside] to the loan amount. This combination of equity and debt is the indicator of business value.

LEVERAGING CASH FLOW[SF]
BELL-Quest, Ltd.

VARIABLES:

Free Cash Flow	$ 19,932
Earning Set-Aside @ 25%	$ 4,983
Capitalization Rate	11%
Annual Debt Service	$ 14,949

Step 1: Calculate Monthly Payments For Debt

Free Cash Flow	$ 14,949
(÷) Payments per period	(÷) 12
Monthly Payments	$ 1,245.75

Step 2: Determine Amount of Financing

Interest Rate	5.5%
Loan Term	15
Monthly Payment	$ 1,245.75
Balance on Due Date	0
Financing	$ 152,463

Step 3: Business Value Indicated

Financing	$ 152,463
(+) Equity [$4,983/11%]	$ 45,300
BUSINESS VALUE	$ 197,763

Note the superscript "SF" refers to the use of seller financing. In the next chapter, a similar superscript "BF" will indicate financing is secured from a bank or commercial lender.

Reality Check

Once the leveraged cash flow calculation is completed, move away from the details to inspect the overall result. Does the indicator of value produce a result that makes good sense? These criteria may help answer this question:

- **Realistic Financing:** Review basic terms of financing to ensure they are consistent with reasonable expectations of the market. Examine length of loan, interest rate and amounts of payment in relationship to free cash flow available. If inconsistent, make final adjustments and recalculate.
- **Realistic Equity:** The business value is the one that will attract the most investors willing to pay the price. Investors want financial leverage. They want a return on equity; opportunities that require more than 50 percent equity with sub-par returns are less attractive.
- **Realistic Value:** With the exception of proven franchises, buyers are justifiably cautious about purchasing too much goodwill. Review the amount of intangibles in the business value. There must be a very good reason for goodwill, in dollars, to exceed buyer's equity. When it does, the opportunity can quickly lose its luster.

Don't Overdo It!

Understanding indicators of value and how to use them leads to making adjustments in variables to affect the result. This is when a person's intellect and integrity can become detached from one another. A seller's desire to justify a higher price might prompt an increase in the term of financing or a reduction in the interest rate charged. The amount of financing that a fixed amount of free cash flow can support is increased to suggest the business can justify a higher price. Reducing the management compensation to increase free cash flow or raising the RPM has a similar effect. As expected, a buyer will do the opposite to reduce the investment indicated. Note the effect of the following adjustments:

Variable	Reduced	Increased
Interest Rate	Raises Value	Lowers Value
Loan Term	Lowers Value	Raises Value
Management Compensation	Raises Value	Lowers Value
Capitalization Rate	Raises Value	Lowers Value
Risk/Price Multiple	Lowers Value	Raises Value

Suppose the valuation variables were changed as follows: Interest rate: 6.5 percent. Loan term to 20 years. Capitalization rate to 10 percent. Examine the effect on value indicated when making these small changes to the levering cash flow technique.

LEVERAGING CASH FLOW^{SF}
BELL-Quest, Ltd.

VARIABLES:

Free Cash Flow	$ 19,932
Earning Set-Aside @ 25%	$ 4,983
Capitalization Rate	10%
Annual Debt Service	$ 14,949

Step 1: Calculate Monthly Payments For Debt

Free Cash Flow	$ 14,949
(÷) Payments per period	(÷) 12
Monthly Payments	$1,245.75

Step 2: Determine Amount of Financing

Interest Rate	6.5%
Loan Term	20
Monthly Payment	$1,256.75
Balance on Due Date	0
Serviceable Debt	$ 167,086

Step 3: Determine Business Value

Affordable Loan Balance	$ 167,086
(+) Equity ($4,983/10%)	$ 48,930
BUSINESS VALUE	$ 216,016

The adjustments increase indicated business value by $19,153 or 9.6 percent! In the real world most businesses are offered with little regard given to justification of price. On those occasions, when an owner has this knowledge, it is clearly possible to manipulate the estimate of value to suit the purpose. A reality check will help reveal the validity of adjustments made. Challenge them.

In the higher value, terms of financing are more favorable than those previously offered. The equity appears attractive, too.

At 23 percent of indicated business value, this creates financial leverage that will stimulate increased buyer interest.

The biggest problem created by the adjustments lies in the relationship of price to goodwill. With tangible assets having a fair market value of $165,000, the value of goodwill is $51,916—more than equity and more than management compensation. This may be unappealing to many potential and qualified investors. Therefore, the adjusted business value, though plausible, could be counterproductive and reduce the number of interested buyers. This does not support the goal of a business owner attempting to sell.

Make adjustments to the variables to refine business value and improve its accuracy. Ensure, however, that they remain consistent with actual marketplace conditions and the expectations of the principals involved. Then put the business cash flow to work for you.

CHAPTER 12

Unlocking the Bank Vault

Why cash is king.

Indicators of Value

When using indicators of business value, it's a good idea to develop a value range using cost, market and income approaches. Combined, these are good indicators of value. When changes in capitalization rates, business operation and financing occur, such as those illustrated in the latter part of the previous chapter, business values indicated often follow suit.

While most businesses that actually sell often involve some amount of seller financing, many do not. The alternative? Pay cash or seek financing elsewhere. As long as entrepreneurs believe in the benefits of financial leverage, commercial lending institutions will remain a viable option.

 INTERNET REFERENCE

www.sba.gov
The U.S. Small Business Administration provides financial, technical and management assistance to help Americans start, run, and grow their businesses. The SBA is the nation's largest single financial backer of small businesses.

http://sbs.dnb.com
The Dun & Bradstreet Small Business Solutions website provides business owners with a suite of online tools to make better credit decisions.

The U.S. Small Business Administration (SBA) is a branch of government established to assist entrepreneurs in most aspects of business start-up, expansion or acquisition. Small business valuation emphasizes financing. Providing services to meet this need is at the core of the SBA's mission. Its activities are varied, however, and support entrepreneurs in other ways as well (e.g., through the Service Corps of Retired Executives—or SCORE—which includes more than 12,400 counselors in 389 chapters nationwide).

Business loans typically involve greater risk than real estate loans. This is because financial benefits and value are a derivative of tangible and intangible assets. Both can evaporate quickly, diminishing their desirability when used as collateral to secure a loan. To encourage lenders to accept the greater risk of financing small businesses, the U.S. Small Business Administration (SBA) offers, under certain conditions, guarantees of payment to lenders making small business loans. Because these programs reduce risk to both the borrower and lender, they increase the desirability of small business loans. When sellers want cash for a business and buyers want to preserve financial leverage, commercial lenders get involved, and, when they do, so does the SBA.

To learn more about participating in the various SBA lending programs, visit www.sba.gov.

Bank Versus Seller Financing

A key difference exists between terms of financing offered from a seller and a bank. This affects the outcome when levering cash flow into equity and debt. One key consideration with the latter is that the amount of financing is determined from loan terms and the amount of debt the business can afford. Typically, 100 percent of free cash flow is committed to retire debt. Sellers are not so concerned about the relationship between debt and the market value of tangible assets serving as collateral.

Bank guidelines are more costly and challenging. These establish the upper limit of credit available to a small business borrower without regard to free cash flow. Debt is determined using loan-to-value and debt-coverage ratios, explained earlier in this text. When combined with other factors, such as interest rate and terms on financing available, a bank lends less than a seller. In some cases, the amount of free cash flow committed to service debt is also less. When this happens, the difference between free cash flow and annual debt service (ADS) on a bank loan may be diverted to pay off a smaller second mortgage to a seller. (Bankers often view the existence of such as a vote of confidence in the buyer from the seller; it can be an important incentive to lenders whose loan approval is wavering.)

To illustrate the immediate impact of bank lending guidelines on available financing, consider the following example.

Loan-to-Value Ratio:	80% for all assets
Debt-Coverage Ratio:	1.2
Assets Market Value:	$165,000
Free Cash Flow:	$19,932
Equity Set-Aside:	$4,938

With this information, a maximum loan available can be determined. To do so, multiply the assets market value by the loan-to-value ratio.

$165,000 x 80% = $132,000 (maximum loan available)

Next, convert free cash flow into annual debt service when discounted by the bank's debt-coverage ratio. This is done as follows:

$14,949 ÷ 1.2 = $12,457.50 (annual debt service)

Note: Cash available for debt service, but not used ($14,949 - $12,457.50), may be considered additional equity set-aside. This amount ($2,491.50) is added to the previous set aside for a total of $7,429.50. The result will be an increased amount of equity contributed by the buyer that tends to be favored by lending institutions.

Divide the annual debt service figure by 12 to determine the monthly debt service. Apply the monthly payment calculated ($1,384.17) to the terms negotiated in order to calculate the loan amount affordable. Assume the interest rate is 9.75 percent and the loan term is 15 years. Here are the variables used with an amortizing calculator to determine the loan amount.

Payment	$ 1,038.13
Interest Rate	7.0%
Term	15
Future Value	0
Loan Amount	$115,497.59

Since the bank has set a debt ceiling of $132,000, the loan amount ($115,497.59) is within limits imposed by the lender and within the cash flow capability of the business.

LEVERAGING CASH FLOW[BF]
BELL-Quest, Ltd.

VARIABLES:

Free Cash Flow	$ 19,932
Equity Set-Aside	25%
Tangible Assets	165,000
RPM	2.57
DCR (Debt Coverage Ratio)	1.2
LTV (Loan to Value Ratio)	80%

Step 1: Calculate Monthly Payments For Debt

Business Free Cash Flow	$ 19,932
Equity Set-Aside @ 25%	$ 4,983
Annual Debt Service	$ 14,949
Debt Coverage Ratio @ 1.2	$ 12,457.50
(÷) Payments Per Period	12
Monthly Payments	$ 1,038.13

Step 2: Determine Amount of Financing

Interest Rate	7.0%
Loan Term	15
Monthly Payment	$ 1,038.13
Balance on Due Date	0
Serviceable Debt	$115,492.15

Step 3: Determine Indicated Business Value

Total Financing Affordable	$115,492.15
(+)Equity ($7,474.50 / 11%)	$ 67,950
INDICATED BUSINESS VALUE	$183,442.50

CHAPTER 13

Home "in" on the Range

More values are better than one.

Value Scenario

Imagine a contest where two archers compete by aiming at a target 200 feet away. Each gets four attempts to hit the bull's-eye. The one judged most accurate will be the archer who places the most arrows closest to the center of the target.

The competition begins, and the first archer hits the bull's-eye with one shot, next misses by an inch, then misses by two or three inches with the other two. Robin Hood would be proud. The second archer misses the bull's-eye first by a half-inch, then twice by 12 to 15 inches, and then the final arrow fails to hit the target at all. Based on these results, the first archer is clearly more accurate. He had a better aim and produced a better result more consistently. One could have more confidence in the winner, especially if he were to act as your bodyguard.

Consider a Range of Values

Measuring business indicators of value, and the confidence we can have in them, is similar to an archery contest. If similar results are created by using several techniques to indicate value, one can be more confident of their conclusions. There are many ways to indicate value: comparable sales, industry rules of thumb and, to be sure, capitalizing business income, calculating a multiple of excess earnings, and leveraging the cash flow into equity and debt with seller and bank financing. If the spread of these values is small, that's good. If, however, the spread of values is large, confidence in the final estimate will be less. In these situations, do more research to find out why the spread of values is wide.

Revisit the valuation variables to ensure they are correct for the situation. Check the math used to calculate each indicator. Reconsider the logic of each indicator of value—a multiple of excess earnings is not always appropriate for a service business with few tangible assets. Stay with it until the spread narrows and confidence grows.

Defining the Range

"Central tendency" describes the general numeric location of a group of results. The mean is the average of a group. The median is the point below and above which there are an equal number of values. For example: In the range of numbers 0 to 10, the median is five because there are exactly five numbers above it and below. And the mean is also [conveniently] five.

The mean and median are useful when working with a range of values because they help pinpoint the most realistic indicator of business value based on several measures used to create it.

In this text an example is used to illustrate how one business can be considered four different ways. Using four common small business valuation techniques, the following range of values is developed. Here are the results.

VALUE RANGE BELL-Quest, Ltd.	
Capitalized Value of Earnings	$ 181,200
Multiple of Excess Earnings	$ 197,143
Levering Cash Flow (Seller Financing)	$ 197,763
Levering Cash Flow (Bank Financing)	$ 183,443

A Simple Analysis

The mean of results, their average, is $189,887. This could be a good estimate of the business value based on four logical indicators of value.

Another approach involves use of the range median. The range—the distance between values at the upper and lower value in the range—is $16,563. And the median—one-half the range added to the lowest value—is $189,482. At this value no result in the range is more than $8,282 from the center of the range. That's a variance of less than 5 percent ($8,282 ÷ $189,482) that also represents a fairly accurate estimate of business value. The formula to produce these conclusions follows.

RANGE ANALYSIS BELL-Quest, Ltd. To Determine Market Value	
Mean Value	$ 189,887
Range	$ 16,563
Median of Range	$ 8,282
Low Value in the Range	$ 181,200
Market Value of Business (Median)	$ 189,482

The close similarity between the range mean and median [$405/.2%] offers added confidence in the accuracy of the final indication of value.

What to Do With the Result

Developing indicators of value, plugging them into a value range, and producing a mean, median and estimate of market value, have little use if not put to work. How this is accomplished really depends on the unique position of the individual doing the work.

Buyers working with value ranges will use them to drive down a seller's asking price. When initial indications suggest it is too high, these tools provide strong support for a price reduction. This is important, because no business is inherently a bad opportunity. Unrealistic pricing, however, can make them so. Thus, it is possible to identify more candidates for acquisition from the pool of available opportunities. The secret is knowing what they are really worth.

Sellers working with value ranges use them to stand firm when buyers come calling. The most delightful experience possible is qualifying a buyer—identifying what they want a business to accomplish in financial terms—and presenting them with an investment that does "exactly that." It is the surest way to find out if they are truly interested or just kicking tires. And if it is the former, rather than the latter, 90 percent of the work to sell and close is already done. What remains is simple confirmation of the obvious.

Value ranges built on logic are hard to defeat.

CHAPTER 14

Investors Raise a Challenge to Buy Low

"Inquire to lead."
—Socrates

Situation Analysis

Limited knowledge of indicators of business value is a hindrance to negotiations. Sellers discourage buyers when they overprice their businesses. Buyers offend sellers when they offer half what the business is worth. Both are uncertain about the actual business value so neither acts logically and could not mount a capable defense of their position. No real progress comes from either approach.

Using indicators of business value is logical and a terrific advantage for investors who want to buy low or sell high without creating a feud.

You Make Your Money When You Buy

Entrepreneurs make money when they buy and collect it when they sell. Buying low has many advantages. It is possible to sell out quickly and recoup most or all of the original investment. The difference between acquisition cost and actual value is an immediate profit. It isn't necessary to spend years building added business value to create added wealth. Some people pay so much that the business they buy cannot be sold to recover their investment for years, if ever. It takes patience, AND the ability to recognize a good value or create one with counter-proposals. Every business has its price.

EFFECTIVE PHRASE

"I'll make an offer, but I always pay less than market value."

This is an effective way to open negotiations with sellers. It reduces their expectations, so they are not surprised or alienated. It suggests that, in the past, other sellers have sold below market value to this buyer who has obviously performed. Plus, it gives sellers a measure of control. They can choose to proceed and hear the offer or not. It is also a test of the sellers' confidence in their business value. Most, out of sheer curiosity, will always want to know what you have in mind. The door is open.

Business indicators of value empower buyers, sellers and the acquisition process. Core issues are confronted head-on. When both parties understand how business value is calculated, it is easier to close the gap between buyer and seller positions, yet the high-spirited competition and negotiations can remain lively and fair. The final outcome is a win-win transaction.

The often-quoted statistic that four out of five business start-ups fail means an equal number of owners fail, too. Their errors begin before a business is acquired. By addressing certain essentials, however, the potential for success improves.

- Understand non-negotiables.

- Know what a target property is worth.

- Communicate value to encourage acceptance.

Non-Negotiables

Buyers should know what they absolutely, positively cannot accept and avoid the unrealistic expectations of exceeding these limits. Moreover, recognizing critical factors of success helps prevent trouble before it begins. Observing non-negotiables is one way this is accomplished. Non-negotiables are things the entrepreneur cannot do without, because to do so makes failure a near certainty. Following are non-negotiables for every buyer's list.

Don't pay too much. Entrepreneurs who start, buy or exchange into a business make this their mantra for life. It is never knowingly violated. When it is, the path to poor results is already underfoot. After learning effective valuation techniques, how could this occur? Adrenaline is powerful. When a live business candidate emerges, the rush of excitement is persuasive enough to overpower reason. It's easy for the heart to overrule the head. Business indicators of value help restore a healthy balance and prevent mistakes.

Remember the Objective

Many entrepreneurs forget to consider an important issue when acquiring a business: Business owners do well and do best when doing what they like most. They have to, because entrepreneurs must be willing to work 16 hours a day for themselves instead of eight hours for someone else. It's not worth the effort, however, if there's no profit in the mix. Buying low ensures this mix is available.

Financial autonomy is the goal. Business is the impetus of the American system of free enterprise. Business ownership is the mechanism entrepreneurs choose to accomplish their goals. Performance leads to profit. Profit leads to choice. Choices lead to freedom. In this quest, business valuation skills offer a useful tool.

Plan to Shop Around

Don't let your endocrine system control your investment process. Keep emotions in check and review opportunities dispassionately. Buying a business is a calculated risk many want to take—few make the effort to think clearly and calculate the risk first.

There are many businesses available for purchase. Some are good opportunities—others are among the four out of five heading for failure. There must be a compelling reason to acquire a business whose trend of trailing revenue and earnings is declining. Instead, find a business that is thriving, surviving, or can be re-energized by identifying and scaling a growth wall in the path of progress. Financial autonomy has a better chance of occurring when a business shows a favorable track record.

Good business opportunities are often overpriced. Sifting through all the opportunities, both good and bad, to find the best value is the goal. But this can be time-consuming, and entrepreneurs are pressed for time. So, the objective of smart buyers is to know what information to ask for, and to ask for it early. The key ingredients of the due diligence provide clues to accomplishing this.

First Impressions

Buyers cannot construct an offer involving a commitment of financial resources without knowing what benefits and income go with the property. That is like buying a property "sight unseen," and it's unwise. Buyers should not be expected to make offers based on innuendo, business potential, and the romance of ownership. They are well advised and rewarded when their focus remains fixed on the economic rewards available.

Conversely, sellers can't be expected to open the books to every buyer expressing a casual interest. Serious intent should be demonstrated. Otherwise, requests for financial disclosures are met with resistance, and rightly so, as buyers could be competitors in disguise, attempting to pick the seller's pockets for competitive intelligence. Requests for an executed non-disclosure agreement may be premature, however. The trick is to find out if both buyer and seller are in the same ballpark.

Consider the power of first impressions. With people they can be revealing and accurate. In fact, everything afterward is an attempt to confirm what is already intuitively known. Business opportunities are similar. It isn't necessary to perform a due diligence to develop a quick opinion of business value. Using basic variables and three valuation strategies help form a reasonably accurate first impression.

KEY INFORMATION

Educate Others—They Don't Know Value

Don't assume sellers and lenders know how to determine what a business is worth. This is a buyer's advantage. Simple questions can be very effective tools. It isn't necessary to teach them to calculate indicators of value. It is important to explain your logic and approach, because you need reliable information and they have it. Remember, ask questions. Inquire to lead.

Reverse Roles

Putting the seller in the buyer's shoes is the easiest way to convey a sense of concern for the business asking price. This leads to uncertainty and confusion. They find themselves looking for a logical way out and that leads to greater flexibility. If it appears the seller is willing to listen to alternatives, illustrate a price that makes sense. If the seller remains inflexible, walk away. And never bluff. Too much is at stake to play games. Say what you mean and mean what you say.

Challenge the Price

Always counter-offer an asking price. Always. This is a seller's opening gambit, and never to be accepted without a challenge. Occasionally a business is available, but no price is stated. This is typically the result of a seller who: 1) doesn't know the value of the property, 2) hopes to find a buyer who doesn't know the value of the property either, 3) has a high standard of confidentiality, or 4) is skilled enough in valuation and negotiating techniques to know better.

The clue to determining the skill of the seller can be revealed with the question, "How was the business value determined?" The answer received will reveal the seller's skill and negotiating capability. If it is consistent with any of the first three cases just mentioned, it is difficult to proceed very far. Financial disclosures will be equally limited. Don't invest too much time. If it appears the seller fits the fourth category, deliver a non-disclosure agreement—this could be a good business, so look closely.

Challenge the Terms

"Are you willing to finance any portion of the asking price?" This is an excellent question to test the seller's confidence in his business. It also helps buyers get a fix on factors motivating a seller to sell. Generally speaking, the word "terms" means financing and its conditions. For reasons described earlier, financing provided by a seller is more attractive to most buyers. Where seller financing is not available, the buyer needs a good knowledge of loan criteria from potential commercial lenders. Investment leverage in business acquisitions can improve the financial return. It will be important to consider the cost to service debt from business cash flow. This is something else a buyer needs to know early.

Challenge the Assets

"What do I get for my money?" is a simple question that challenges sellers and tests their confidence in business value. Typically, responses describe the various assets included in the business and their market value. Goodwill, if it exists, is difficult for sellers to include. This approach allows a buyer to add asset values and see if their collective total matches the business price. In this process, any price paid for goodwill is revealed. The subtle challenge to a price continues setting the stage to buy low.

The question about assets has another benefit. Buyers need to know the type and amount of collateral available to secure financing from a bank. It puts a seller on the defensive by challenging the asking price of the property being sold.

Challenge the Revenue and Cash Flow

A request for details like revenue, EBIT and cash flow threatens a seller more than broad-based inquiries. Asking for business revenue is broad and shouldn't create unfavorable exposure. More importantly, getting revenue opens the door to inquire about trailing revenue that reveals business trends, which is important to the valuation process.

EBIT (earnings before interest and taxes) is a little more difficult to secure. Sellers maximize expenses to minimize taxable earnings. The problem is they may not be able to articulate it confidently or explain how it is accomplished. Go easy and help them understand what you need and why; e.g., there is a difference between net profit and cash flow.

The goal at this point is to estimate business cash flow. It is easy to follow up with a request for additional limited information leading to EBIT. Then more limited questions can lead to development of cash flow. For example, "Was there a depreciation expense? A salary for your management effort?" are good questions that, surprisingly, create added interest in the seller to go along. Add a request for monthly cash expenses (rent, utilities, insurance, payroll, etc.) and, if received, estimate the business's cash flow. Better yet, just ask for the financial records and circumvent the need to be a sleuth!

Challenge the Management Compensation

Most buyers know how much income from employment they need to support their lifestyle. It is always helpful to know what existing ownership believes management compensation should be. This is not a threatening request. Compare answers to the employment income tables in the U.S. Bureau of Labor Statistics website. They can confirm estimates made and provide the basis to challenge them.

Challenge the Price with Capitalization

Buyers who accept a business asking price without a challenge let sellers to do their thinking for them. This is a lazy, dangerous approach and very easy to avoid with the right skill. It pays to be a skeptic. Buyers demonstrate a healthy sense of skepticism by challenging representations made, such as the asking price. This is the easiest and most obvious way to negotiate a lower sales price. The reason more buyers don't take this approach is because they are unable to use indicators of value to justify a different position—they have nothing on which to base an argument. For this reason, indicators of value are powerful tools.

The simplest way to challenge an asking price is by capitalizing the income using your own predetermined capitalization rate. Assume the following from the example of BELL-Quest, Ltd., used in previous chapters:

- Asking price: $300,000
- Free cash flow: $19,932
- Business capitalization rate: 11.0 percent

Begin the challenge by using variables provided by the seller—price and cash flow—to figure the rate of return. Free cash flow is $19,932. The equation to determine the rate of return (free cash flow divided by the asking price) becomes:

$$\$19,932/\$300,000 \quad = .0664 \text{ or } 6.64\% \text{ rate of return}$$

At the asking price of $300,000, the rate of return to an investor is 6.64 percent. This is less than the expected capitalization rate of 11.0 percent. At the asking price, the business does not offer a competitive rate of return. This is not good news to a seller.

"If you back a seller into a corner, be prepared to show him a trap door to the treasure chamber."

Next, calculate the amount of income that should be available from an investment of $300,000 producing the expected rate of return. Substitute an 11.0 percent capitalization rate and recalculate:

.11 (11.0%) x $300,000 = $33,000 (Free Cash Flow)

To produce the desired capitalization rate, the income (free cash flow) should be $33,000. The actual amount is $19,932, or 40 percent less based on market indicators of performance. This is another indication the business is overpriced.

Finally, calculate the adjusted current business value by using current free cash flow and the expected capitalization rate:

$$\frac{\$19,932}{.11\ (11.0\%)} = \$181,200 \text{ (Indicated Value)}$$

Based on these criteria, a buyer can determine <u>the business is overpriced by roughly $118,800!</u>

💬 EFFECTIVE PHRASE

"Would you buy this business for that?"

The analysis and question is fast, easy and revealing. Wide discrepancies in asking price and value are commonplace. With this information the buyer now can terminate the inquiry or, if the only apparent problem with the business is the price, attempt to negotiate it lower. In either case, time and money can be saved.

Another productive approach is to ask the seller to explain how the price of $300,000 was constructed, or request additional information to shed new light on the issue. This yields valuable information. In the absence of meaningful evidence or willingness to listen to reason, don't waste too much time. Move on.

Challenge the Price with Excess Earnings

A second way to challenge the asking price is by applying the multiple of excess earnings method to confirm a business asking price. A business RPM (risk/price multiple) is needed. This is difficult to do without the benefit of a due diligence. Circumvent the process (early in the inquiry) by interviewing the seller. Explain how an RPM is created and ask the seller to assign a simple value of zero-to-five to each basic category used to build an RPM. These can be challenged later if a due diligence indicates a need for adjustments.

If a seller is unwilling to provide this assistance, the buyer can make a general estimate of the values leading to an RPM. Bear in mind, however, this means a seller is showing an unwillingness to even talk about the business he wants to sell. His motivation may not be very high.

Begin with variables that are known or can be calculated from what is given. Free cash flow is $19,932 and market value of tangible assets is $165,000. First calculate the value of excess earnings using the asking price and value placed on tangible assets included in the business offering:

$$\$300,000 - \$165,000 \quad = \$135,000 \text{ (excess earnings)}$$

Thus, the asking price includes $135,000 for excess earnings or goodwill. Next calculate the RPM needed to support this investment. Recall, excess earnings are the same as free cash flow. Working backwards to calculate a business RPM is easily accomplished.

$$\frac{\$135,000}{\$\ 19,932} = 6.77 \text{ (risk/price multiple)}$$

A 6.77 business RPM is off the scale that measures small business performance. It could occur only in a very hot seller's market or when a business has almost no margin for error or risk. The exceptions are very fast-growing companies in a hot industry with crazy prices and equally silly buyers. Assuming conditions are more normal than this, ask the seller, "How is $135,000 for goodwill justified?" Based on the response received, terminate the analysis or, as before, indicate the need for evidence to support use of such a high business RPM.

Challenge the Price—Levering Cash Flow

Levering cash flow is the acid test. It shows the business can perform at asking price or it cannot. Other measures of value are good, but this challenge measures the investor's ability to afford the price and is telling. To complete this challenge, one must know the cash flow ($58,722) and cost of debt service, which as offered is $2,022.36 per month (or $24,268 per year) to finance $225,000. Calculate management compensation:

$58,722 - $24,268   = $34,454
(cash flow for return on equity and management compensation)

Perform a sanity check. Management compensation is deficient to expectations of the USBLS surveys ($38,840) by $4,386, or 11 percent less. This is a problem, because it may not enable buyers to support a reasonable lifestyle. That would disqualify the business as an investment candidate. In addition, there is NO return on buyers' equity of $75,000 (25 percent of $300,000). NO return. Finally, the goodwill is a whopping $135,000! This business price is too high for expectations.

To calculate the best price by levering cash flow, return to the previous equation and subtract appropriate management compensation from cash flow. Next, deduct 25 percent for equity set-aside. The remainder is free cash flow that can be used to service debt—annual debt service. Divide free cash flow by the number of payments made per year (12) on financing. This is the monthly payment available to service debt. Then recalculate the present value of the debt using the monthly payment. This reveals the amount of financing the business can afford to pay. Finally, calculate equity by capitalizing the equity set-aside at 11 percent to get the result produced in the previous chapter.

The Right Price

The shrewdest investors follow the simplest approach. They identify the price at which the business value meets their expectations. They communicate their position clearly and firmly. Then they stick to their value and negotiate—giving away things that don't really matter. In each case, the result is the same. Profit is earned the day ownership is transferred.

Entrepreneurs following these strategies know they do not need to buy every business to be successful. Be patient. Wait for a good opportunity. It is important to invest in only good values. A business purchased for the right price can produce enough profit to compensate entrepreneurs for a year's worth of earnings. It is worth waiting for. A bad deal can be equally costly and is worse than no deal at all.

CHAPTER 15

Sellers Rise to Challenges and Gain Control

Never let anyone put you on the defense.

Preparation = Control

Control is important. Buyers attempt to wrest it away from sellers with challenging questions they think sellers are unprepared to answer. They will put a seller on the defensive. Uncertainty grows. The seller becomes more malleable—willing to adjust the price. This is costly. Advance planning and preparing good answers are the best ways to take control of negotiations.

To avoid selling too low, successful sellers and brokers prepare to deal with the expected and unexpected aspects of selling a business. It can be a complex process but achieves good results.

Begin by preparing answers to questions a well-informed buyer may ask. Many were presented in the previous chapter. Here are effective counter-phrases to use while putting in motion the all-important strategy of taking the lead. Remember, no single question will make the sale. Work instead to improve the percentages—the chance—that a sale will occur. Here are ten common questions buyers ask and effective phrases that counter them.

Request #1—"I'll make an offer, but I always pay less than market value." The best response is, "That's fine; let's talk about your offer." This approach is a signal the seller is open to everything but not too weak to accept anything. Keep in mind, to a buyer, less than market value could be 10 percent less. This might be a good opportunity. Find out what the buyer has in mind before turning them away by showing a lack of confidence.

Request #2—Respond to the question, "Are you willing to finance any portion of the asking price?" with, "It's possible with a good offer from a qualified buyer." This tells buyers they will be expected to make disclosures, too. A credit report and financial statement are the most common. If these are not acceptable, and buyers know it, they fade quickly.

If financing is not a possibility, the better response is, "We had not planned to offer any financing. Local banks are available to provide that." This doesn't exclude financing as a possibility. It diverts the buyer inquiry to an alternative source. Exercise caution when suggesting other sources of financing. If you elect to provide any contacts, suggest several without making a recommendation.

Request #3—"Give me nickels and dimes." This is a metaphor to illustrate the way some buyers won't relent in their requests for small concessions. This can start in the first meeting. Sellers who respond by agreeing to "this, then that" place themselves at risk. Individually, these items may have little value. Collectively, and when combined with a low offer, they can add up to a princely sum. Buyers will take the position that the seller also has "already agreed to" the concessions, to make things more difficult.

Respond to requests for numerous small concessions with, "We will be happy to discuss that in negotiations." This indicates a willingness to discuss the proposition but requires that the buyer show more cards—go farther into the process—to get an answer. In other words, "Get serious or get lost." The more he investigates, the more he will sell himself—get emotionally involved with the business. Asking for little concessions will be harder, especially if the price is well justified.

Request #4—"What do I get for my money?" should prompt the immediate response, "Income, assets and a marketing opportunity—what any good business offers." Only a continued investigation to develop information describing each—a due diligence—will provide the answer. This is a process any seller can control to gain a negotiating advantage. Release information judiciously.

Request #5—"Can you tell me what the business earns before interest and taxes?" is a question to describe business earning power—a key issue. Answer with revenue, net profit and EBIT. Emphasize favorable business trends if they exist. Don't rely too much on describing potential unless tangible evidence to support increases in performance already exist. This is a good occasion to counter with questions about the buyer's capability—"How much of an investment do you have available?" is an excellent follow-up response.

Request #6—"How did you arrive at the asking price?" Challenges to price are all avoided when the business value is realistic. The best response will indicate value is a function of estimates using a market, cost and income approach. Do not, however, share these estimates with a buyer at this stage. The ability to do their own "homework" is an indication of their capability. Lead the way. Then, make the business available by soliciting offers. This gives buyers a sense of freedom to set their own price but challenges them to stay honest.

Request #7—"Can I look at your books?" This is a common request buyers make to ensure they are not wasting their time. It's reasonable but usually premature. Respond with, "I'm happy to offer them as a condition of an acceptable offer. Until then, know they will verify my disclosures." This keeps discussions moving forward and engenders confidence while bypassing the issue until a full review of the books is warranted. This also is a good occasion to mention that, in exchange for a look at the books, buyers will need to provide a signed non-disclosure agreement and, perhaps, their financial statement. So, have an NDA prepared by the attorney and have it on-hand. It lets buyers know this is serious.

Request #8—"Will you discount for cash or take less?" Many buyers use this as a way to test a seller's confidence in the business value and set the stage for a low offer. For example, a buyer might establish that the price will be less because they plan to offer cash. Then when the offer is tendered, it includes seller financing, but at the cash price. A good way to handle this is by saying, "I'm happy to react to anything you care to propose in writing." This avoids suggesting a lower offer is acceptable and forces buyers to perform if they want more information.

Request #9—"How much are you skimming?" There's only one answer: "None." Skimming is illegal. Any answer damages the credibility needed to create the confidence a buyer must have to buy the business.

Request #10—"Why are you selling?" This is a good question all buyers should ask. Unprepared sellers can offer an answer that may reveal serious weaknesses and place them at a negotiating disadvantage. That's what the buyer wants. There are many correct answers, but one of the best is, "To cash in my equity and reinvest elsewhere." This is a strong answer that fits many situations and suggests the seller is not in a distressed situation.

Selling high also involves other preparations that can favorably affect negotiations. Here are several areas to address.

Conduct a Due Diligence

Sellers can control the negotiation process by controlling the information. One way is to anticipate a buyer's reaction to the business by performing a due diligence prior to a sale. Material in this book is intended to help readers do this themselves. There are three objectives to consider.

First, identify the business strengths and weaknesses. This helps guide the effort to reinforce problem areas. It also points out benefits sellers sometimes do not see, which can be emphasized in a sales marketing plan.

Second, performing a due diligence improves objectivity and expectations. This will be especially true if the opinions of others are solicited confidentially. A list of consultants whose input may be valuable includes professionals already serving the business (i.e., accountant, lawyer, insurance agent, and banker). They do not always need to know the purpose of the due diligence. It can be positioned as an annual review. Their unbiased remarks help sellers see their businesses for what they really are.

Third, the due diligence will include developing a business RPM. This can be used to calculate value with the excess earnings and leveraged cash flow methods of business valuation. That is a key benefit. Additionally, an RPM constructed under these low stress conditions is likely to be better considered, objective and accurate. That is an important resource when a buyer challenges it with one of his or her own.

These preparations are part of an overall strategy that does not give a buyer a reason to say "no." When the time comes, this advance preparation will help a seller stay focused on running the business while negotiating its sale. Maintaining a calm, confident and organized state of mind at that time is sure to be perceived as strength.

Price

Price is one thing over which sellers have total control. The extra effort to prepare a business for sale pays big dividends in a price that can be substantiated and received. It takes time to do this job right, but the work is small compared to the years of work it takes to build the business. This is all of little value without a final effort to maximize the wealth created. Preparation is the key. This aspect for the seller's consideration is most important and, fortunately, the one over which sellers have the most control.

When developing a business price in anticipation of a sale, several things are up for discussion. The objective is to weigh the following elements carefully and create an attractive offering.

A Seller's Biggest Mistake

Don't overprice the property. History indicates that uncertainty about business value often drives up asking prices. This is a reaction to the fear of selling for too little. Leaving "room to negotiate" is not an unreasonable tactic until the room becomes the size of a gymnasium. This strategy then creates more damage than it was designed to avoid. An unrealistic price cannot stand up against the sound logic of a well-informed buyer with penetrating questions.

Overpricing a property discourages buyers from pursuing an inquiry beyond the initial phase. Lots of good inquiries lead to attractive selling options. With fewer buyers in tow, options are limited. The inclination is to take "whatever is available" and an unreasonably strong position quickly softens. The consequence is sellers are easily placed on the defensive, and the outcome can be a sale of the business below market.

Best Time to Sell

The bulk of this book is designed to illustrate indicators of value. The question of "how much?" is easily answered, but "when to sell?" is another question of some importance. It has an easy answer, too. The best time to sell a business is just before its value reaches a peak. Knowing your marketplace and your business provides clues to when the peak will arrive. Unfortunately, this also is when most sellers refuse to let go. By this act they could be letting go of a capital gain from a sale whose economic value could be greater than another two or three years of business income taxed at ordinary income rates.

Prior to a business peak, all systems are go. Trends are positive, as trailing revenue and earnings are steadily increasing. The business enjoys a high profile compared to past activity. Skills that permit business owners to successfully manage the enterprise enable them to predict the near-term future, including how high a peak will be, when it will arrive, and how long it will last. If the business is offered after the peak is reached, the trend starts to flatten and isn't as positive. Value declines.

Buyers normally chase profits. When the trend of business is positive, buyers are more attracted and optimistic. They expect the peak to be farther away than it actually may be. As a result, they are more motivated to act, they will extend themselves a little further, and their offers are a little sweeter.

Measured Responses to Create a Productive Sales Environment

Informed buyers build a strong case to support their opinions of business value. They will attempt to get sellers to justify a price. A different set of issues creates anxiety for the novice buyer. He or she can want a lower price without knowing why. In either case, a seller's response sets the tone for continued discussions, if any. It is important to gauge that response, so it is consistent with the situation. Following are a few suggestions for sellers to improve the negotiating environment:

- Don't overreact. Keep an open mind, review the conditions and try to understand the buyer's position. Remember, many buyers are inexperienced entrepreneur wanna-bes. They may be representing themselves at the bargaining table. Like sellers, the buyers try to protect themselves; they do this with a very low offer. They might be willing to offer more if they could understand why it is justified. It may be necessary to educate them.

- Don't offer a reaction to a first proposal except to listen. The first objective is to understand the specific terms and conditions. Learn what there is to work with.

- Go slow. Never hesitate to "sleep" on a proposal. This is a reasonable request. A few hours can produce remarkable changes to an initial perspective. First impressions are helpful—but the details can often change a first impression. Aggressive expiration dates with an offer are a buyer's attempt to take control of the situation. Ignore them if they are unreasonable.

- Always get something in exchange. Never give buyers anything without receiving something in return. Put buyers on notice early that everything they want comes for a price. It begins with a request for information. Request a non-disclosure agreement first to see if they are serious. Requests for free training might be countered with a request for compensation as the instructor. Remember, buyers will stop asking for more only when they discover there is a cost associated with these requests.

- Convert opinions to offers. Any buyer interested enough to challenge an asking price is usually an interested buyer. He or she might ask small questions to see how much a seller is willing to negotiate. Shrewd buyers often make verbal offers to test the seller's confidence in the price.

Here is a word to the wise: "Verbal offers are not worth the paper they aren't written on."

- Under most conditions a buyer is not obligated to honor a verbal offer. In the give-and-take of negotiating, by responding to a verbal offer, the seller indicates a willingness to negotiate and gets little in return. Treat verbal advances as an opportunity to encourage a written offer.

 EFFECTIVE PHRASE

"Entrepreneurs work 16 hours a day for themselves to avoid working 8 hours a day for someone else."

The rewards of business ownership are more than money. Sell the business lifestyle. Remind the buyers why they want to buy. They want to work for themselves. They want to be in charge of their days and their destiny. They want to have their own business investment. They want to build wealth. Illustrate this by giving examples of how these benefits are things you get to enjoy by owning the business you are selling to them. Emphasize favorable business trends. Don't delve too far into specifics of how the price is calculated.

A simple response to a verbal offer testing the business price or terms is to inquire whether buyers are willing to put it in writing. If they are, wait until they do. In other cases buyers may attempt to negotiate peripheral issues verbally, too. Make notes. When buyers see things put in writing, even as casually as notes, they get more serious. Indeed, putting things in writing can strengthen buyers' resolve and commitment to perform.

Each small piece of information given to a buyer may mean little if considered separately. Together they build a compelling case to support value and contribute to an overall sense of urgency to buy. When that happens, challenges have been met, head on, and sellers can stay on the offensive.

CHAPTER 16

Plan Ahead to Sell High

Don't put faith in the three Ps:
1. *Put up a sign.*
2. *Place an ad.*
3. *Pray.*

The Most Important P: Preparation

When a legitimate buyer shows interest, nothing is more impressive than sellers with all the facts at their fingertips. Business owners are equally empowered when prepared to act quickly.

Assemble Documentation

There are many documents that can be prepared well in advance of a sale. These include but are not limited to the following:

- The company business plan (current year)
- The company marketing plan (if written)
- Corporate resolutions to list and sell the property
- Certificates of good standing for a corporation
- Descriptions of all personal property
- Fictitious name registration
- Descriptions of real estate with legal description or a lease
- Negotiated options to extend the real estate lease
- Good photographs taken on a clear, sunny day
- A blank note, security agreement and mortgage or deed

- A checklist of things to do after a buy/sell agreement is accepted

- Request forms for credit references and a buyer's personal financial statement

- A blank bill of sale

- A title report on the real estate (showing it is marketable)

- A current franchise operating circular and agreement (if applicable)

- Competitive market analysis or intelligence

- A list of vendors and key contacts

- A customer list

- Samples of marketing materials, advertisements, and press clippings, etc.

These and other forms and documents will permit a seller to act as fast as a buyer.

KEY INFORMATION

Ensuring that a fictitious name registration is in place may seem excessive. It is not. Buyers have been known, in the absence of such a document, to register the existing business name in their own name. Their next move is to approach the owner with a demand they cease using their existing business name because it is not their property, or lower the asking price. Imagine such a prospect, and the negotiating power it could create. Don't let it happen—plan ahead.

These preparations are part of an overall strategy that gives a buyer no reason to say "no." When the time comes, this advance preparation will help a seller stay focused on running the business while negotiating its sale. Maintaining a calm, confident and organized state of mind at this time is sure to be perceived as strength.

Explain & Prove Performance

Anticipate a qualified buyer's request for financial documentation to justify the asking price. Any attempt to finance the purchase price (at a bank) will automatically trigger a request for three to five years of business financial statements and tax returns. What if the buyer doesn't understand the difference between net profit and cash flow? To be safe, along with financial statements, build an ERCON (earnings reconstruction) for the past three to five years, too. For each of these years, illustrate the difference between net profit and cash flow. From this it is possible to show trends in trailing revenue, costs and earnings.

KEY INFORMATION

The biggest mistake sellers can make: overpricing their property. Some may think it's underpriced and taking a hit. When the property is underpriced, it usually sells. The seller receives something. When overpriced, it doesn't sell quickly—maybe never sells. As a result, the property languishes on the market for years, perhaps, and then can't be liquidated. This produces nothing for goodwill that earlier might have justified a reasonable value.

Consider a Buyer's Need for Income

It is also a good idea to estimate management compensation since this has an effect on business value (and is used in all valuation methods). Complement that information with input from local sources. Consider keeping this information private, however, since buyers may be willing to pay a lower level of compensation than a departing seller who's had it all to him or herself.

Forecasting

Predicting business results that are yet to come is a difficult thing to do. The best advice is *don't*. If a business is sold "proforma," or if the forecast was to produce certain results and it doesn't, a buyer is sure to be dissatisfied. Buyer's remorse is powerful. It is better to let buyers do their own forecasting.

Alternatively, in the presence of a strong business trend, selling from a forecast might be justifiable. In addition to the ERCON, it is possible to construct a one-year forecast of revenue, net profit and cash flow. The company accountant can help. This forecast needs to be as accurate as possible. The success of buyers who are financed by a seller will depend on the quality of the forecast. The goal is to try to identify business "momentum."

For purposes of valuing the business to sell, however, the following are realistic approaches to consider. Business momentum, using trends and a forecast, can be used to build a value range. This is like a buyer's value range but with a small difference. A seller's value range uses business market values created from the current year and a forecast of next year's financial results. Assuming business is increasing, take the average of values calculated from these results (this year's value and next year's value). This becomes an asking price.

Alternatively, if the business is not cyclical but trending up, one might forecast the next twelve months of results from the month most recently completed. Either approach keeps the seller from overpricing the business.

This tactic raises the price, though not so high as to be considered excessive. Buyers will determine for themselves if the asking price is "about to be" justified. Caution: When forecasting earnings, keep these private—marked "not for distribution." When appropriate, give buyers enough information to prepare their own forecasts. Trailing results and basic trend analysis of historical results are sufficient. Otherwise, a seller's forecast of future results can be interpreted as a promise of what is to come. There are no guarantees.

Target Buyers Pay Most

Two types of buyers exist for a business. The best sales strategy to attract one or the other is to identify which can derive the most benefits from the business offered. Because they have different objectives, this should be taken into consideration when deciding the right benefits to emphasize.

The most frequently encountered small business buyers will be owner/operators. They are interested in buying a business and operating it personally. They want employment income and the ability to service acquisition debt until paid under reasonable conditions. A marketing effort to attract this buyer should emphasize these benefits. It will also paint a picture of the creative fulfillment available from ownership, since this is a co-benefit of some importance—the sizzle of the steak. Remember, this buyer wants to become free if currently employed. Show the buyer how buying this business can make it so.

The second, less common, type of buyer is an investor or financial buyer. This buyer is making a business investment and does not want to run the business. This may be a practicing entrepreneur, or a larger business on the prowl for good acquisitions. Either seeks growth by non-organic means—to buy instead of build. To them the creative fulfillment of business ownership is less important; financial results are the priority. Recall, the owner/operator wants employment income—management compensation will be an important issue, alongside free cash flow to service debt. Investors will be concerned about these points too, but the acquisition is less personal. These buyers normally hire someone else to manage the business. Also, most investors are looking for opportunities that offer synergy.

The ability to reduce the costs of management compensation, administration, marketing and production can have a dramatic improvement on net profit. Moreover, these types of buyers often have more cash and may not need financing. Therefore, free cash flow is measured as a return on investment of cash. As a result, price may be a function of the capitalization rate selected. Investors are more aggressive and select high cap rates. The acceptable asking price can go up when synergy is present.

If synergy is added to build cash flow, savings occur and improve free cash flow. This can be estimated. The business value can increase because the benefits justify more. For example, suppose synergy creates a savings of $20,000 in the expenses of Bell-Quest (our example) so, for this investor, synergy improves the free cash flow from $19,932 to $39,932. Now assume this investor uses a more restrictive capitalization rate, say prime times three [5.5% x 3] or 16.5 percent. Using the capitalization of income method indicates the value of Bell-Quest, to this particular investor, is now $242,012. That's an increase of $60,812 over the value calculated with the lower cap rate and free cash flow! Does it include more goodwill? Absolutely! But it is very saleable. Investors recognize the value of intellectual capital. When the numbers fit, they are more willing to act.

Sellers need to decide early which type of buyer is most likely to be attracted to their offering. The defining criterion is, surprisingly, not always good financial results. Investors seeking to grow by acquiring more of what they already have may pay a reasonable price. More is paid for acquisitions with synergy and unique, productive intellectual capital. With a few price comparisons, it is possible to target the right buyer.

Make a note: While investors may sometimes pay more, they can be harder to find and tougher to sell. A business must have a high cash flow to successfully attract a premium from them. In most cases, the small business opportunity with fewer than 10 employees is best suited to meet the needs of an owner/operator. But take heart; there are about 15 million businesses in that size category and approximately 90 million Americans who want to own one of them. The odds favor those who plan ahead.

CHAPTER 17

Business "Sale by Owner" Strategies

Don't give buyers a reason to say "no."

Smart Move or Misconception?

Is selling a business without the assistance of a brokerage professional an effective strategy? This is commonly called a "for sale by owner" approach. Most who choose this method of sale wish to avoid paying what they perceive to be a large brokerage commission. They believe they know their business well enough to sell it themselves and they think they have the ability to advertise their business "confidentially" to keep their intentions a secret. All of this is plausible, but not as easy as it sounds.

Business brokerage commissions of 10 percent are common—it can cost thousands to sell a business. Those who choose "sale by owner" might expect to get the job done for less. It is possible: However, a support team is required to help sell a business—and they don't work for free.

Another misconception is that sellers know their business better than anyone who may attempt to sell it for them. This is a misguided assumption. Most sellers know how to sell their goods and services to make a business profit. Selling the entire business, however, is a very different kind of "goods or service" and requires a different type of skill, which most sellers don't possess. This phenomenon is often discovered too late by those attempting to franchise their business. Running a business that sells and serves franchises is not the same as operating a franchise.

Finally, sellers know how to attract buyers to their business to buy what they sell. Attracting buyers to buy the entire business requires a different approach. Many sellers are not well-schooled in how to attract buyers, confidentially, to buy a business.

Still, many business owners sell their own businesses. Those who succeed usually have a good plan of action to follow. This helps keep the business sales process from becoming a distraction to running the business. Unfocused effort produces poor results. Sellers who want to sell their own business should begin by remembering three things every seller really wants.

1. The Highest Price

A business's highest price is the value buyers are ready, willing and able to pay—today. The highest price is a recognizable value. It is easily justified, offers reasonable management compensation, a return on equity, and can support acquisition financing required. The highest price attracts lots of buyers. Try to imagine how much easier it is to negotiate potentially lucrative finer points of one offer when three other offers are in play. The old rule is, "While you're writing offers in the stock room, keep talking with buyers in the conference room."

Knowing a business's highest price is a more important issue to sellers planning to market the business themselves. They don't have time to speculate; their time is limited. While a business is on the market, the owner's interest costs (if any) and other related direct and indirect holding costs continue. These can have an unfavorable impact on business performance and sale price. So the highest price is joined at the hip to the time it takes to sell a business.

2. The Shortest Time

When most entrepreneurs decide to sell, they want it to happen yesterday. This is because a new business vision, inconsistent with current conditions, may already be in place in their minds. Under these conditions, ownership's focus is distracted and management effectiveness is often diminished. This is a bad combination of events and can be costly. Standards of performance decline, and new opportunities are missed. The entrepreneurial spirit that drove the company to success is diminished. Burnout can easily occur.

When a property is available for a long time (more than six months), the owner can also become frustrated with the sales process. This is natural and easier to deal with when one knows what to expect. Frustration is greater if ownership's intent to sell does not remain confidential. Employees are not blind. Learning the boss is selling out may encourage them to consider employment elsewhere. Employee turnover has significant direct and indirect costs. New employers must be found and trained before becoming productive—another distraction. Customers learning of the business sale may notice changes, too, and take their business elsewhere. When attempting to sell, the timing of these reactions could not be worse.

The combination of factors described can negatively affect revenue, expenses, net profit, cash flow and the business value. Worse, intelligent buyers who notice a business languishing on the market will take longer to act, hoping the price will fall farther. Clearly, the situation can be grim for the unprepared. There is, however, a solution.

Working behind the scenes, sellers can anticipate and develop a complete business disposition strategy. It takes six months, a year or perhaps even two to maximize the results, but it can be worth the effort.

3. The Least Effort

Face it. Selling a business is not always easy. It is unwise to assume the one-in-a-million buyers with money to burn will magically appear. It is better to prepare for a well-informed buyer. Also, don't be too focused on finding a buyer who wants to own and operate the specific type of business you offer. Small business buyers will generally entertain a variety of small business types, provided they represent a good investment value. This should help widen the pool of buyers who can be attracted and increase the chances a sale will occur. Beginning with a good preparation to sell in place, the sales process can be set in motion. Selling your business can be accomplished with a series of small incremental steps taken over time that considerably reduce the effort expended. This strategy works best.

KEY INFORMATION

Time on the market is correlated to preparation. When a business offering is well planned and available at a reasonable price, a sale occurs much faster. This is because capable buyers know a good deal when they see one. They also know it won't last. Good sales plans and pricing strategies engage a buyer's sense of urgency to act. Building a sense of urgency among buyers makes the seller's job easier.

To begin a sale by owner process, create a detailed plan of action—a sales plan. Successful sellers do their thinking early to ensure better execution later. Here are seven strategies of successful business sales plans. It goes without saying that all are preceded by the important task of creating a well-justified business value.

Selling Strategy #1: Assemble and Use a Support Team

Many attempting to sell their own businesses ask whether or not they should engage others to help them and, if so, how much they should pay. Selling your own business is a team effort and often includes the business accountant, attorney, an advertising professional and, in some cases, a broker. Each can play a meaningful position on the team, but the seller must assume responsibility as its captain. Make contact with each team member before you begin.

Accountants—A good accountant can help organize and prepare financial information that will be meaningful to buyers. Most already understand how a business is valued and can confirm the work performed by a seller. This can save lots of money. Accountants can also provide statistics about similar businesses to support investment value. Also, buyer confidence in a business opportunity grows when buyers inspect financial records printed on an accountant's stationery.

Lawyers—These professionals fulfill the valuable function of translating agreements into writing. This will include non-disclosure agreements, letters of intent, offers to purchase, and all closing documents. They have escrow accounts that can be used to hold deposits and sales proceeds. This is all a necessity. Lawyers also have the secret handshake that is often required.

It is common for buyers to engage the services of an attorney to represent them in a transaction. It's the smart thing to do. It is unwise for a seller to attempt negotiating directly with an attorney; retaining a lawyer to stand in for the seller improves negotiations. Lawyers can talk to each other, get things done, and move the sales process forward.

Advertising & Public Relations Professionals—Advertising professionals can help plan a campaign to advertise the business. Their copywriting experience enables them to write energetic advertising copy that will attract buyers. Knowledge of the industry gives them the ability to recommend newspapers and alternative publications where effective advertising can be placed. They know the goal of advertising is to generate leads, not sell the business. Using their skill will accomplish this important objective.

Public relations experts can plan, write and release press releases about a business to local media. They can position business owners as local experts on pertinent topics and important news sources. This strategy raises the profile of the business. If local buyers exist, this may attract their attention without the exposure of local advertising.

Brokers—The goal of selling a business directly to save a brokerage commission doesn't mean a broker couldn't act as part of a team. Brokers are a valuable resource. Utilizing them as consultants paid by the hour can be very helpful. It is an option every business owner should seriously consider. They may offer benefits that outweigh the cost.

Brokers already know the market, and competent ones can quickly evaluate the desirability of a business opportunity. They can make objective recommendations to improve the process and the result. For a flat fee, or an hourly rate, they can meet regularly with sellers to ensure they are staying with the plan. Plus, if results are not achieved, brokers can become "Plan B." Brokers already may have created many marketing mechanisms needed to promote the sale of a business. They may be linked with qualified buyers waiting for a good opportunity. In such cases it could be less costly to pay their commission than to proceed alone. Under the right conditions, using a broker can be a real savings of time and money.

 **KEY INFORMATION**

Use the Bluebook Appendix B

Refer to the section titled "General Terms and Features of Acquisitions" for more information on the sales process. This section includes helpful explanations of key issues, conveniently arranged alphabetically.

Selling Strategy #2:
Advertise Confidentially

Every seller wants to advertise his or her business to every buyer on the planet while keeping it a secret. This is not possible. Nevertheless, any plan to successfully sell a business will involve some form of advertising. It is possible to let the word out in ways that do not disturb the confidentiality sellers crave. Effective advertising in other geographic markets often accomplishes this feat.

Very often the best buyers for a business are not local. This will be particularly the case in rural areas. Local (in this case rural or suburban) investors' historical bias disqualifies them. The local buyer remembers when the business offered was started or purchased years earlier for much less, inhibiting the ability to think in terms of current-day values. Also, local investors already are located in the market; moving to a new location is not a motivating factor.

Out-of-area buyers don't have the historical bias. They want to relocate. This is especially true of those attempting to move from the city to the country. In an environment where jobs are scarce by comparison, buying a business in a small town is a powerful lure. Properties a local buyer wouldn't take on a bet could be a city buyer's dreams come true.

Effective advertising would include placements in classified sections of newspapers serving regional metropolitan areas. Target those areas that seem to be the former homes of local residents. This rule of thumb also is a practical way to select a city in which to advertise your business. *Buyers often move from north to south and from east to west.* That's because business buyers are far enough along in their careers to be looking for a better climate, less congestion and a simpler existence.

Blind advertisements are those that describe the business without revealing its identity. Use descriptive phrases like "low-stress lifestyle" to make a business sell like the smell of bacon. Give basic information only and set up a post office box to receive inquiries. Many newspapers can provide this service for a small fee.

Selling Strategy #3: Qualify the Buyer

A well qualified buyer can perform. The capabilities of a buyer who has not been qualified are questionable. It takes a great deal of time to sell a business; don't waste it on buyers who can't perform. The quickest way to qualify buyers is by asking them to sign a non-disclosure agreement early. Buyers who are serious, motivated, well informed and capable will understand the need for this. They have nothing to hide if the request for the non-disclosure is linked to an additional request for "like-kind" financial information, such as a financial statement at a later date.

Unqualified buyers will balk at these requests. Also, determine the buyer's objectives. It will be helpful to remind them of these as the negotiations continue. Determine their investment criteria to help create a fit between them and the business. Until there is a fit, it is unlikely a sale will occur.

KEY INFORMATION

Buyers Are Expensive

It can cost hundreds, even thousands of dollars in time and effort to attract a buyer ready, willing and able to buy a business. When buyers surface, don't let them get away. It costs more to find a new buyer than to keep working with one already on the scene. The key to keeping a buyer interested—and making efficient use of advertising dollars and ownership's time—is to qualify them accurately. Use this information to avoid giving them a reason to say "no" to acquiring the business.

Qualifying a buyer is a specific skill that often takes years to learn. But you can learn it quickly by taking a simple approach. Just attempt to get to know the buyer before attempting to sell him your business. It is essentially a chance to see if the principals' values mix well or create sparks. With good chemistry and shared values, it is more likely a sale can be negotiated. One good way to test for buyer and seller chemistry is with a phone call between principals. Another is a simple meeting during breakfast or lunch in a public restaurant. Both of these venues provide a neutral environment.

When qualifying a buyer, pay less attention to what he wants and more to what he needs. This is important because buyers ALWAYS want to talk about and focus on things they want from a business and NEVER use these as a basis for investment. Sellers must be shrewd enough to distinguish a buyer's wants from his needs. The qualifying process is the time to determine what they are and which is which. The decision to buy is nearly always based on the latter: NEEDS.

For example, a buyer who needs $50,000 of management compensation from a business to support his family may go on and on about the nifty product line or location of your business. He may speak endlessly about being his own boss for a change, as well. But he will not buy a business that has everything he wants if it doesn't have enough compensation to meet his income needs.

Don't be afraid to ask these and other questions. Qualifying a buyer can save a lot of time working with people unable to perform. It can also help tailor a transaction to suit the buyer's needs. Keep the discussions rolling by accentuating the positive and deferring discussion of potential deal breakers while successfully negotiating smaller issues.

EFFECTIVE PHRASE

Qualifying Questions You'll Want to Ask a Buyer

1. Why do you want to buy a business/this business?
2. Do your spouse and family support business ownership?
3. What sort of work do you do now and have you done in the past?
4. Are you buying for yourself or another, and do you have any partners?
5. How much annual income are you accustomed to earning?
6. How much equity—cash—do you have available, t day, to invest in a business you want to buy?
7. Will you need financing?
8. What interests you about my business?
9. What are some other objectives you want to accomplish by acquiring your own business?
10. If you find a business that meets your criteria today, are you prepared to take action now and buy it?

Selling Strategy #4: Give Buyers What They Want

The typical buyer profile is a person who wants to buy a business and become self-employed so he can escape from a dead-end job. He wants the business to offer reasonable financial leverage with a modest down payment. Business cash flow should be sufficient to pay off the acquisition debt in a reasonable amount of time. Don't let your ego take control and suggest it takes a degree in rocket science to successfully operate your business. Make it seem simple. In summary, the business should be easy to buy, easy to pay for, and easy to run. Structuring the sale of a business with a price, terms and benefits that accomplish these objectives provide a much greater chance of selling.

Selling Strategy #5:
Do Things for Buyers
They Cannot Do for Themselves

This is the first rule of successful selling. When executed it makes a seller more valuable to a buyer. This makes it easier to lead a buyer through the sales process.

> Milton Erickson was a famous psychologist who treated patients using the power of a paradox. He learned his craft early on the family farm. One day he was observing his father attempting to pull their bull out of the barn. No matter how hard he pulled on the rope around the bull's neck, the animal only resisted more and moved backwards. Young Milton asked his father if he might try to move the bull. He began taking the rope and gently walking around the bull, turning him so he was facing into the barn. Then, he pulled on the rope with all his strength and the bull backed out of the barn. The moral of the story is, "You can manipulate me all you want just so long as I like it."

Typically, when attempting to buy a business, there are three things most buyers cannot do for themselves. These are: 1) justify the business value, 2) secure financing, and 3) take the next step. Justifying business value is easy to do if the business is properly priced. One needs to know only the buyer's basic income needs to illustrate how the business earning power can meet them. Securing financing is easy if a seller wishes to finance the sale. If sellers want cash, a well justified price will also make it easier for a buyer to secure financing from a bank. The third is a result of inexperience that, typically, is not a problem for sellers. Help buyers take the next step by leading them through the acquisition process. This helps secure their confidence and trust. Both are required before they will write a big check to buy a business.

Selling Strategy #6:
Control the Flow of Information

Generally, buyers want to know everything about a business without offering anything, such as an offer, in return. It's called a "free look," something sellers should avoid. Give buyers enough information to create added interest and develop the lead. The objective is to "keep the mystery alive" so it is possible to keep giving buyers more of what they want.

The basic structure of a business sale will involve receipt of a valid, enforceable non-disclosure agreement from buyer to seller. This occurs very early and before any "substantial" information about a business is shared. Next, the buyer is given access to limited information about the business (not financial statements but a summary of business results). Also, the buyer is granted access to a one-on-one with the seller to discuss the details of a business.

After disclosures have been made, and if the parties agree to proceed, a formal offer to purchase should be prepared. Once executed, buyers may conduct a thorough due diligence to verify what they have already learned. Upon completion of this process, and satisfaction of any contract contingencies, the parties proceed to close.

KEY INFORMATION

Honor the Evidence Room

Use the "evidence room" approach to distribute key information. Once a buyer has indicated sufficient interest to pursue an acquisition, and signed a non-disclosure agreement, set up a meeting between principals. At this meeting the seller should bring confidential summaries of business results, business operations, etc. The buyers might also bring their financial statements. At this meeting each is free to question the other about matters of importance to an acquisition. They can inspect documents brought to the meeting. They may not copy them. At the end of this meeting all parties take with them everything they brought. Thus, the information is available for inspection only in "the evidence room." Using this approach helps parties to a transaction get to know one another better without unnecessary exposure to either.

Selling Strategy #7:
Avoid Distractions

Selling a business while running it can be a major distraction. The reason is running the business might have become boring while selling is charged with new excitement. Those who sell their own businesses must keep their eyes on the ball—maintain revenues and profits so they don't decline. If that happens, the desirability of the business will fall. Here are three especially nasty distractions to avoid:

Burnout—Many successful careers have ended in burnout when all that was needed was a week off. If burnout is a problem, take time off to get a fresh perspective. It may seem like a costly thing to do, but the price can be small compared to allowing revenue decreases that result in a substantial reduction in business value.

Siren's Song—Some buyers, especially those from a larger company, may show interest in acquiring the business. An inquiry from a source such as this can easily engage the ego. It can be a destructive path to follow.

Larger businesses often grow by acquisition and, thus, are very experienced. They know the first step is to get the seller's ego engaged. Their initial inquiry often proposes to give the seller "everything he wants." There is great danger here. Sellers can spend so much time and energy working with their "big buyer" that they forget to tend to their own business. Buyers detecting this slow-down trend start taking away small things they originally proposed and allow business revenues to decline. The original business value, now more difficult to justify, becomes less. Very frequently, a formal offer is finally submitted that is far less than the original "intentions" expressed. The seller is now stuck with the options of selling for less, starting over with another buyer (also at a lower price), or rebuilding a business they are attempting to sell.

Straw Parties—Many buyers—and this is especially true of a competitor—will use a "straw party" to advance their interest to buy a business. A straw party is a person who has no apparent connection to the real buyer behind the scenes. This is done for two basic reasons.

First, a large company with considerable financial resources doesn't want to reveal its interest. The concern is that sellers realizing this interest will "raise the price." Hence, they attempt to work in secret. A non-disclosure agreement is often sufficient to prevent this problem.

Second, some competitors simply want to learn all they can about the business with no intention to buy. This is an attempt to "pick someone's pockets" for free. It can be very damaging, too. After the buyer inquiry fades, rumors can be released that the business is for sale. This can unfavorably affect business revenue and cause employees to become concerned. With the use of a properly worded non-disclosure agreement, this situation also can also be avoided.

CHAPTER 18

Tactics to Boost Business Value

Remember, after building value beyond your wildest dreams...the goal was to sell.

Your First Consideration

When buying or starting a new business, selling should be the last subject on one's mind, right? Wrong. It should actually be the first. This is because one wants to make the business worth as much as possible. Build value starting on day one; don't wait until you want out. When you know the factors, or variables, that most affect value, you can make profitable decisions from the start—and you'll get the highest possible price when the time comes to sell.

Well, that's just great you may be thinking. *I've been in business for years...is it too late for me to ensure getting a good price when it's time to sell?* Relax. It has been shown it does take time to get in a position to sell profitably. Normally, you'll need a year to prepare before putting your company on the market. This way you'll have time to take some tangible steps and make your business more attractive to potential buyers.

As discussed earlier, selling out is best supported by a good sales strategy. It gives buyers a sense of urgency to take action and make an offer on what appears to be a great deal. Here are specific tactics that help business value and motivate buyers to act quickly.

Tactic One:
Location, Location, Location

Secure the business location because it facilitates customer traffic that leads to sales, profit and, ultimately, higher business value. Develop assurances the location won't change after the sale occurs. Here's how:

If the property is leased, renegotiate the terms with options to renew. This will provide added security for the potential buyer.

If you own the real estate occupied by your business, consider refinancing it to withdraw your equity. Increasing your cash reserves will be helpful during the selling process and, if the buyer wants to acquire the real estate too, the financing is already in place.

Tactic Two:
Develop an Internet Presence

This is a second business location on the World Wide Web. It can bring more traffic to your business and has promotional value. A website can increase revenues during the year before a business is offered for sale. And higher revenues translate into a higher selling price. A proactively managed website also creates the impression you are "in the game."

Tactic Three:
Create Curb Appeal

Dogs don't sell very well. A business that looks like a dog tells a buyer there's lots of deferred maintenance to be performed. That will take cash that might otherwise be used to buy the business.

Clean up and fix up your business before you make it available for sale. Make it shine, both fiscally and physically, by selling off dated inventory, attending to repairs or equipment needs, and releasing nonessential personnel and replacing them by outsourcing, if possible. This way, when a buyer comes calling, there's little to do other than take over. The amount the buyer can invest can be greater, and it increases your business value.

Tactic Four:
Reduce Uncertainty

Most sellers are afraid to tell employees they will be selling the business because of unfavorable reactions and early departures. You can reduce this uncertainty by periodically reminding staff that every business asset owned is for sale every day you own it. Prepare yourself to make financial disclosures a buyer will want. Have your accountant build a business cash flow analysis. Keep updated contracts with employees, consultants, clients and customers. Don't give buyers a reason to say no. "Nolo Supre Prendre"—No Surprises!

Tactic Five:
Stop Skimming

An old saying goes, "The difference between tax evasion and tax avoidance is five to ten years in jail." Skimming happens when a business owner receives income but does not report it for income tax purposes. Skimming is tax evasion and it is illegal. Plus, it reduces the business income, profit, and value. If you skim, stop. You'll eliminate tax and legal entanglements, and the bottom line and business value will improve. Remember: "Skimming is that portion of the business price you take before you put the business up for sale."

Tactic Six:
Build a Succession Plan

A buyer may be unsure of his or her ability to run your business after the sale. You can assure him or her by offering a training program, which includes a timetable to explain the basics of how your business works and a plan for the seller's involvement, which should gradually cease, usually within about 60 days.

Tactic Seven:
Become More Visible

There are two times to increase the business advertising budget in business. One is when business is terrible and your competitors can't afford the cost. Then you can increase market share at their expense. The other is when you plan to sell out. More advertising prior to a sale of the business increases the public's awareness of your business. It's a subtle way to attract a buyer's attention. This is important because someone in your marketplace is likely to be your buyer. The more they see your name, the greater their perception of your presence in the marketplace. This increases their perception of your business's value.

A strong public relations effort will further compliment the effort to build the image of your business prior to a sale. Become a local expert for your industry. Do this by presenting valuable information to your community via press releases, talks, or visits with local clubs. Offer your knowledge as a news source to area media outlets. Try to find a news story from your industry that would be of interest to their audience. People trust the industry experts. Trust builds business value.

Tactic Eight:
Eliminate Weaknesses

Prepare a brief summary or an extensive review of your business. Either way, it must be done in preparation for a sale. You can hire a business valuation analyst or do it yourself, with step-by-step guidance from this book. Perform your own due diligence. Develop your own pricing multiple in the process. From this exercise you will identify the strengths and weaknesses of your business.

Restaurant operators might focus their attention on ways to lower food costs in order to increase gross profit. Manufacturers that eliminate deferred maintenance by refurbishing equipment enable buyers to commit more cash available to buying their business. Retailers can sell off dated inventory for a modest discount instead of selling it for cost or less when included in a sale of the business.

These tactics eliminate a business's weaknesses and build its strengths, thereby creating a more desirable, secure investment opportunity.

Tactic Nine:
Identify Synergy

All buyers want to find synergies in businesses they buy. Synergy has a favorable impact on business results. It makes the business investment more attractive. When synergy exists, the business price can be higher than when it does not and must be developed. Recognizing the types of synergy your business has will enable you to target a specific category of buyers who will pay the highest price.

Buyers who want to run a business look for situations where they can use their skills. For example, if you are selling a retail business, don't think about selling it to a person retiring from a manufacturing job. They like being left alone and would have little interest. This is important to remember if financing the sale. Such a person could quickly develop distaste for customers and acquire a personality like sandpaper. The business will not fare very well under their ownership. Collecting on your note could become questionable.

Instead, sell to people familiar with sales professions. Leveraging existing knowledge to run a business reduces the learning curve. A shorter learning curve leads to improved performance and results. Identify the critical types of work a buyer must perform to successfully run your business. Then try to identify a source of buyers that would possess these skills. They will be more attracted to the business and pay a higher price.

Investors—financial buyers—buy businesses for raw earning power. They want a return on their money. Frequently, they own other businesses and their motive is to combine the costs of certain expenses such as accounting, legal, advertising, procurement, location, shipping, etc. This is the type of synergy they often seek. In many cases they buy businesses to increase the buying power of several businesses. Purchasing in larger quantities often results in greater quantity discounts. The retained price, however, may remain unchanged. The difference saved is added profit. Some of this difference can be used to justify a bigger business value.

Tactic Ten:
Structure More Than One Transaction Option

Develop alternative sales options so your business can appeal to a larger array of buyers. For example, sell for cash or finance the property yourself. Sell the business and keep your business real estate—lease it to the business buyer. Or, sell the business and place the real estate into an IRC 1031 tax-deferred exchange. Various selling options will create the flexibility needed to accommodate the investment capabilities of a larger number of buyers. The odds of selling increase.

Regardless of the option you select, remember to qualify the business and the buyer. Qualify the business by selecting a pricing strategy that makes financial sense to a buyer. No buyer can succeed who buys a business priced so high that the chances of making a profit are virtually eliminated. With a realistic price, it is possible to offer seller financing or sell for cash. Then qualify the buyer to ensure he has the financial capability and professional skill to run the business successfully. Remember, a qualified buyer can pay more.

Tactic Eleven:
Establish a Clear Title

This seems like such an obvious tactic that many dismiss it. That can be a big mistake. Unfortunately, many have the unpleasant experience of discovering just prior to a closing there is a problem with the title to the property. This is why, long before the closing occurs, title companies conduct searches of property ownership and encumbrances. If any problems exist, they can be removed before the eleventh hour. An even worse problem exists with companies involving extensive software services.

Companies using computers and proprietary software to provide a service are unusually vulnerable. Many business owners are not aware of the rules involved when working with computer programmers. When a programmer is hired to build a program, known as a "writing code," for a company, he gets a fee in exchange. The fee paid, however, secures the payer only the rights to use the code, perhaps exclusively, but does not convey a right of ownership to that code. Consider this. It is possible to pay to have programmers build an extensive and very expensive software solution. But without proper conveyance of ownership, it is not possible to pass clear title to this "code" to a new owner. The liability is this: The programmer could show up at the closing table looking for a check that represents "his share" of the proceeds for "his property" being sold.

The scenario played out in a software services company can happen with photographers and writers, too. So it is wise to have an agreement with consultants that clearly transfers and assigns their ownership rights to all they create for the business in exchange for getting paid.

Tactic Twelve:
Avoid Burnout

Curiously, many small business owners overlook the hard and soft costs of extended sales effort. They can be substantial and far greater that the difference between a price that is too high and one that is realistic. Many entrepreneurs sell because of burnout. And yet, from this negatively charged state of mind, they are forced to continue operating a business while simultaneously launching a typically covert marketing effort to sell out. If overpriced, the business can languish on the market for more than a year.

When a business is experiencing owner burnout, negative thinking may have an unfavorable impact on revenue and profit. If competitors discover a sale is contemplated, they may attempt to bleed off customers so more revenue is lost. Still worse, key employees who learn of an impending sale may become insecure and seek employment elsewhere. Employee turnover costs are often one to two times their annual earnings, so operating costs rise.

Burnout, loss of confidentiality, and customer and employee turnover all contribute unfavorably to business performance. The final sales price often decreases as the time it takes to sell increases. Selling the business separately helps prevent this unpleasant phenomenon.

All these tactics are within the grasp of most business owners. You can't put them to work, however, unless you can measure their impact on value. A proper valuation is the lynchpin of any effort to boost business value.

CHAPTER 19

Parts Sold Separately... for More

When separated, a business and its real estate might bring a greater value.

A Unique Opportunity

Ownership of both a business and the real estate it occupies is common among small business entrepreneurs. This arrangement often results in a special situation when it is time to plan an exit strategy. In essence, both properties may be available when it is time to sell out. Ownership frequently attempts to sell them as a package deal for one price. Valuable marketing and income benefits might be realized, however, by offering these properties as separate investments.

Waxing Philosophic

Typically, entrepreneurs start or buy a small business first. They are driven by a desire to work for themselves at this early stage of entrepreneurship. The business opportunity is the primary target. A different motive is involved when making a commercial real estate investment.

Later, during the evolution of ownership, wealth building and continued business security emerge as dominant issues. Additional business assets are often acquired to support these objectives. Acquiring the real estate occupied by the business is one of the more obvious acquisitions entrepreneurs entertain. This move can build wealth and ensure continued access to a proven business location—

a key ingredient of predictable business success. When it is time to sell, however, entrepreneurs are well advised to consider unwinding their business and real estate in stages rather than all at once.

Create a Buyer's Market

When it is time to sell out, business owners want three things: 1) the highest price; 2) in the shortest time; and 3) using the least amount of effort. Offering the business and real estate separately may be the best approach to realize these goals.

When business assets are divided, the price for each will be less than the total of the two. A lower business price will attract a larger number of buyers. More important, a greater percentage of these buyers are likely to be qualified to make the investment. As a result, the ability to solicit realistic offers improves and, with it, the strength of the seller's negotiating hand. Chances are good that a better price will be received.

Experience shows that with a reasonable marketing effort there is an inverse relationship between the pool of buyers created and the time it takes to sell. More of one means less of the other. As mentioned earlier, when a business and real estate are priced together, the higher price disqualifies thousands of would-be buyers. It takes longer to sell when the supply of buyers is limited. Alternatively, when a business is offered separately from the real estate, for a much lower price, the number of capable buyers grows. It takes less time to sell.

Instilling a sense of urgency to act in legitimate buyers is crucial to selling a business. After comparing prices of small businesses, many knowledgeable buyers become adept at recognizing a good value. With the real estate included, a business offering may not be as attractive an investment as it might be without the property. This is because businesses typically produce higher returns than commercial real estate. When the enterprise is offered separately, it's return is not dragged down or diluted by the lesser-performing property. The economics of the business offering are more attractive and will motivate buyers. When a motivated buyer arrives on the scene, less effort is required to negotiate the sale.

Separate the Real Estate and Business Values

Separating a business and its real estate involves both legal and financial considerations. Many times the real estate will be held in a small private corporation that can make the process less complicated. If not, it may be necessary to sell only the business assets and keep the real property. Legal counsel and a tax advisor should be consulted to help determine the best approach.

The Real Estate

The following example will compare and illustrate the impact on financial results when a strategy to sell a business and its real estate separately is applied.

Calculating the value for the business real estate is not difficult. Local market professionals use comparative market analyses to develop fairly reliable estimates of property value. If desired, qualified real estate appraisers can provide added input to reduce uncertainty. When a real estate value is established, it can be subtracted from the price for both property and business. Here is a new range of values to illustrate this adjustment. (For this example, assume the real estate has a market value of $105,000)

VALUE RANGE BELL-Quest, Ltd. For Business When Real Estate Is Subtracted	
Capitalized Value of Earnings	$ 76,200
Multiple of Excess Earnings	$ 92,143
Levering Cash Flow (Seller Financed)	$ 92,763
Levering Cash Flow (Bank Financed)	$78,443

Using measures of central tendency, the market value indicated is $85,887 (mean) or $84,482 (median).

Simply subtracting the value of real estate from business value does not, however, address the issue of affordability. How will cash flow be affected by rent to be paid on the building? And how much should that be? These are important concerns that prompt a more detailed approach.

Determining the value of a business from its intrinsic qualities is a little more involved but may yield favorable results. A limited supply of business appraisers makes it more difficult to secure this information. Where available, their services can be quite costly. If the business is small, it may not be cost effective either. Business comparable sales are of little help because the number of cases to consider is often too small to be useful. Where a larger sample can be found, additional problems may exist. Out-of-date information, lack of similarity to the subject business, and a remote location of cases in the sampling of comparable sales may prevent the analyst using this approach to accurately extrapolate business value.

Accurate Variables Lead to Reliable Values

Consider determining business value by using a combination of indicators of value: capitalizing income or earnings; a multiple of excess earnings; and levering the cash flow into equity/debt using seller and bank financing. Start by assembling a set of variables.

- Real Estate Market Value: $105,000

- Inventory @ Cost: $55,000

- Fixtures & Equipment: $5,000 [Market—not Book Value]

- Cash Flow: $58,772

- Safe Rate of Return: 4.50 percent

- Capitalization Rate: 13.75 percent—Note, now at two and one-half times prime. Removing real estate increases risk by excluding a significant tangible fixed asset, and, by limiting occupancy to lease negotiations.

- RPM: 2.06. For the same reasons the capitalization rate was increased, this is decreased—by 25 percent.

- Financing: One valuation method relies on financing to establish business value. Terms are adjusted to be consistent with shorter class life of assets used to secure business acquisition debt.

Next, minor adjustments to the cash flow are necessary. A reasonable rent expense for the property occupied by the business must be included in the business expenses. Sometimes the amount sellers charge themselves [when they also own the real estate] is far below market value. On other occasions, rent may be omitted entirely as an operating cost. Now, because the real estate is to be excluded from a sale, rent must be estimated and treated as a business expense. But at what amount?

One way to determine rent is to review rates offered for similar business space per square foot. Then apply this factor to determine the market value of space provided by the business real estate being retained and leased.

Another technique to determine property rent for the subject property involves treating the income required on the investment value of the property as rent. Assume a capitalization rate on the building of 6.5 percent. This is less than a business cap rate because there is less risk involved; however, it is still 1 percent over a prime interest rate.

Next, calculate the ROI indicated from a commercial real estate investment worth $105,000 at the selected capitalization rate. The income should be $6,825. This figure will be treated as rent on the building and applied to the earnings reconstruction as below.

Reconstructed Business Earnings

Using either approach, the increased rent expense appears as a negative adjustment in a reconstructed profit and loss statement. This illustrates the variance between business taxable income and cash flow. In cases where the separation of assets occurs, sellers normally offer business buyers a triple-net lease for the real property. The lessee pays all property insurance, taxes, repairs and maintenance. Since these expenses are often included in profit and loss statements, it may not be necessary to make an additional adjustment to business cash flow. Adjusting for increased rent reduces cash flow and free cash flow (cash flow less management compensation) by an equal amount.

EARNINGS RECONSTRUCTION
BELL-Quest, Ltd.

Revenue	$ 608,951
Cost of Goods	<390,190>
Gross Profit	$ 218,761
Expenses	<$ 189,501>
Net Profit	$ 29,260
Interest	$ 4,533
Taxes	----
EBIT	$ 33,793
Depreciation	4,809
Amortization	1,668
EBITDA	$ 40,270
Owner's Salary	18,000
Non-Recurring Expenses	502
Building Rent	<6,825>
Net Adjustments to EBITDA	$ 11,677
CASH FLOW	$ 51,947

Recall the cash flow was $58,722. The difference [reduction] is building rent. Cash flow is reduced to $51,947. Next, estimate and deduct management compensation to determine the business free cash flow—its earning power. When the business cash flow is adjusted for management compensation of $38,840, free cash flow becomes $13,107. Now apply this and other variables to a valuation formula to estimate a new business value.

Capitalizing the Income

Recall the cap rate for a business is 11 percent. Thus:

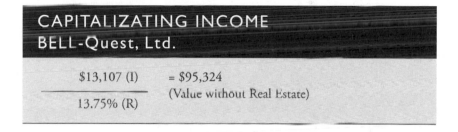

CAPITALIZATING INCOME
BELL-Quest, Ltd.

$$\frac{\$13,107 \ (I)}{13.75\% \ (R)} = \$95,324$$
(Value without Real Estate)

Multiple of Excess Earnings

Using this method requires creation of another important valuation variable—a risk/price multiple. An effective approach to developing this value involves rating key areas of business operation. These are: finance, control, marketing, sales, production, and service. Sub-elements of each may be rated on a scale of 1-5 where the higher number indicates less risk and better value. The average of all sub-elements and all key areas have produced a business RPM that is 2.57. For the same reason the capitalization rate was increased (removal of real estate), it is assumed the RPM will decline slightly. For the purpose of this exercise, the value will be reduced by 10 percent to 2.31.

MULTIPLE OF EXCESS EARNINGS
BELL-Quest, Ltd.

VARIABLES:

Free Cash Flow	$ 13,107
Safe Rate of Return	4.5%
Tangible Assets	$ 60,000
RPM	2.31
Business Free Cash Flow	$ 13,107
Tangible Assets	60,000
Safe Rate of Return	4.5%
Return on Tangible Assets	<2,700>
Business Excess Earnings	10,047
Risk/Price Multiple	2.06
Value of Excess Earnings	$ 20,697
Value of Tangible Assets	60,000
ESTIMATED BUSINESS VALUE	$ 88,697

Levering Cash Flow

Recall, this indicator of value has two variations. Both are designed to provide an indication of business value by determining a reasonable amount of financing a business can pay using free cash flow after a return on equity is set aside.

One variation of the leveraged cash flow method involves the use of commercial financing. This option is not considered for this exercise because the debt coverage ratio (DCR) and loan-to-value (LTV) ratios will reduce financing significantly. For example, an LTV of 50 percent on inventory and furnishings makes only $30,000 of financing available. Financial leverage is lost unless a seller offers secondary financing. Under these conditions, it is more likely a seller will finance the business investment. Seller financing terms, typically more generous than a bank's, are used.

LEVERING CASH FLOW
BELL-Quest, Ltd.
(Seller Financing)

VARIABLES:

Free Cash Flow	$	13,107
Equity Set-Aside @ 25%	$	3,277
Tangible Assets	$	60,000
Capitalization Rate		16.5%

Step 1: Calculate Monthly Payments For Debt

Annual Debt Service	$	9,830.25
(÷) Payments per period		(÷) 12
Monthly Payments	$	819.19

Step 2: Determine Amount of Financing

Interest Rate		5.5%
Loan Term		7
Monthly Payment	$	819.19
Balance on Due Date		0
Serviceable Debt		$ 57,006.78

Step 3: Determine Business Value

Affordable Loan Balance	$ 57,006.78
(+) Equity ($3,277/13.75%)	$ 23,469.09
BUSINESS VALUE	$ 80,475.88

Market Value

Recalculating values without real estate will produce the following value range.

CALCULATED VALUES BELL-Quest, Ltd. Without Real Estate	
Capitalizing Income	$ 95,324
Multiple of Excess Earnings	$ 88,697
Levering Cash Flow (Seller Financed)	$ 80,476

Using measures of central tendency, the business market value is estimated to be $88,166 (mean) or $87,900 (median).

RANGE ANALYSIS BELL-Quest, Ltd. To Determine Market Value	
Mean Value	$ 88,166
Range	$ 14,848
Median of Range	$ 7,424
Low Value in the Range	$ 80,476
Median Value	$ 87,900

Reality Check

The mean business value is $88,166. Subtracting the real estate value ($105,000) from the value of business and real estate ($189,877) suggests a business value of $84,877. Sold separately the business may be worth *$3,289 more!* Moreover, this latter business value is equally likely to pass the valuation tests of educated qualified buyers.

The real benefit, however, is the value of the business. Consider how many buyers are qualified to invest $189,877 versus $88,166. Keep in mind; these are buyers attempting to purchase a business, not investment real estate. As a result, the number of qualified buyers increases with reductions in the perceived investment cost. Consequently, more buyers lead to the increased possibility that a sale will occur. That is the real objective.

In addition, notice what happens to the value of goodwill. If sold as a package, the FMV of tangibles is $165,000 leaving $24,887 for goodwill. Sold as a business without real estate, the goodwill is $28,166—*$3,279 more!*

The business price without real estate still offers the seller plenty of equity, income from reasonable financing (if seller financing is elected) and lease payments on the building. In the future, this stream of monthly payments can be used to justify the sale of that asset to another investor. More likely, however, the buyers of the business will seek to acquire it themselves.

Develop Alternative Sales Options

Separating a business from its real estate can make both properties a more attractive investment offering. Marketing resources expended to sell a business are more effective when there is a target buyer in mind. Generally, there are strategic and financial buyers. This strategy can be used to attract either. More importantly, with the concept of selling the business and real estate separately, and the potential target buyers for each defined, a wider variety of sales options becomes possible.

Sell the Business/Hold the Real Estate

Burnout often associated with the desire to sell a business should not be allowed to affect the investment in its location. The benefits of commercial real estate ownership include cash flow, tax incentives, amortization and appreciation. Performance leases, remaining depreciation, amortization and a location in the path of progress may make holding the property a wise move. Simply sell-ing the business may not erase these benefits. Sellers may want to hold the real estate and decide whether or not to sell it at a later date.

Holding the real estate after selling the business can also be an efficient tax strategy. Selling the business this year and the property in a later tax year may help hold down capital gains income. If this reduces marginal tax rates, an attractive tax savings may occur.

Build in a Buyer for Both Properties

For all the reasons a seller acquired the business first, and the real estate later, a new owner may do the same. The opportunity to set the stage for this event is presented when a business is sold and the property is leased to the buyer. By including a percentage lease rent rate, the cost of occupancy will increase if the business grows. At some point the business operator may realize that owning the property would be less costly. Acquiring it becomes an obvious strategy to pursue. An option to buy at a predetermined price for-mula, or a first right of refusal in the lease, helps make this possible. In the mind of the business buyers, they have already laid a future claim to the property.

Sell the Business/Exchange the Real Estate for Another Investment

It may be possible to sell the business, creating cash, and ex-change the real estate for like-kind investment property. This would be done when the business seller wants to remain active in the in-vestment market but has exhausted the benefits of the current hold-ing. Internal Revenue Code Section 1031 (IRC 1031) specifically deals with the exchange of investment property. The tax code lan-guage is straightforward: "No gain or loss shall be recognized on the exchange of property held productive use in a trade or business or for investment if such property is exchanged solely for property of like-kind which is to be held for productive use in a trade or busi-ness or for investment."

Knowledgeable real estate investors have used IRC Code Section 1031 exchanges for many years to avoid capital gains tax on the sale of real property. The advantage of tax deferment available to owners of real estate is also available on the sale of personal property. While exchanges of real property are more common, sellers of business assets can exchange into a more desirable or profitable replacement property without losing their equity to capital gains taxes. Because a lifestyle change, or retirement, is often a motive to sell their business, this tactic works best with the real estate.

A purchase and sale agreement should contain language establishing the exchanger's intent and notifying the buyer of the exchange. Examples when selling are, "It is the intent of the Seller to perform an IRC Section 1031 tax-deferred exchange by trading the property herein with a qualified intermediary. Buyer agrees to execute an Assignment Agreement at the request of the Seller at no additional cost or liability to the Buyer." With this language in place, the seller of the investment property may proceed to execute the remaining requirements of a tax-deferred exchange.

To illustrate the potential value of a tax-deferred exchange of the real property, assume its fair market value is $105,000 and the adjusted basis is $58,167. Long-term capital gains rates vary for most investors based on the applicable federal depreciation, appreciation and state tax rates. A range of from 20 percent to 25 percent is common, thus, a blended rate of 22.5 percent is used for the following illustration.

Fair Market Value of Real Estate	$105,000
Adjusted Basis	<58,167>
Taxable Capital Gain	$46,833
Applicable Tax Rate	22.5%
Capital Gains Tax	$10,537
Taxes Deferred as Equity	$10,537

Combining the benefits of an asset separation strategy ($3,279) with a tax-deferred exchange ($10,537) increases equity after a sale/exchange by $13,816.

Sell the Property/Hold the Business

It is amazing that so many entrepreneurs succeed at the improbable task of building a business without ever knowing what it is worth. The valuation of a business separately from real estate often uncovers hidden potential. With this new information, some sellers become re-energized enough to continue developing unrealized growth potential. This may require cash. Holding the business while selling the real estate and leasing it back is a common tactic. With a track record of favorable business performance, investors are likely to have greater confidence in the financial capability of a tenant. A premium for the real estate is often paid. Sales proceeds can be invested to stimulate continuing business growth.

Separation of the real estate from the business is a powerful strategy that accomplishes many objectives. It makes a property more marketable, saves valuable time, and has the potential to increase business value. It is a special situation all business sellers who own a business and its location should strongly consider.

Rochelle Stone, President and CEO of Starker Services, Inc., contributed to this chapter. Starker Services is America's premiere Tax-Deferred Exchange third party intermediary with representation in 23 states. They may be contacted at their headquarters in Los Gatos, California, by calling 800-332-1031.

CHAPTER 20

Service Businesses: Worth More Than Many Realize

Make the intangibles tangible.

Small But Profitable

In a recent edition of *A Report to the President*, the United States Small Business Administration estimates 60 percent of all home-based businesses are service businesses. Plus, 53 percent of all businesses are home-based. This rapidly growing sector of business growth is adding significant value to our economy. These individual enterprises—the small service businesses—have value, too. In fact, service businesses—professional and labor-intensive—can carry an impressive value, and they can be sold for a handsome profit.

What's Different About Service Businesses?

Many think it is not possible to sell a consultancy, catering business or window-washing service. This is because they don't have an abundance of tangible assets that investors and lenders rely upon as collateral. In the absence of collateral, a perception exists that the price or value is all goodwill. Not true. A business with a steady cash flow is desired and has value—perhaps more than one with plenty of assets and no cash flow. You can still place a real value on your enterprise. Unfortunately, most entrepreneurs, *especially* in the service industry, have no idea what their business is worth. The old rule of thumb suggests using a multiple of revenue to determine value has some merit if that multiple is derived from a good base of comparable sales. However, recall from Chapter 1, to be meaningful, comparable sales must be similar, here and recent. The list of qualifying comparable sales is likely to be small, and, therefore, using them to build an accurate rule of thumb multiple can be risky. This is important to remember when it's your money being received or paid.

Steps to Reveal Value

The most important point to remember when attempting to cash in your goodwill (by selling out) is: "Do things that reveal a service business's value." Fortunately, many of them already exist, so you only have to put them on display. Value is created when it can be shown how intangible assets—also called intellectual capital or, more commonly, goodwill—make a tangible contribution to business performance. Intangible assets are your reputation in the community, the knowledge of how your business is run, your secret recipes, your skilled staff—the list goes on. The challenge is converting these intangibles into tangible assets a buyer will want to acquire. Do this by revealing or institutionalizing them so there is a perception that they are tangible. This way when you leave the business, revenue doesn't walk out the door with you. Here are some easy steps to consider:

Convert client lists into contracts—Which is worth more: a business with 200 client names or one with 200 client contracts? You may have a steady flow of customers, and those who return often, but neither you nor a buyer can accurately assess the future revenue in a service business. Change that by offering clients a 5 percent discount to sign a contract for a year with a 30-day exit clause. They have little to lose and you have much to gain: more committed customers and a greater perception of business value. It's a smart business decision to ensure income and will make your business far more appealing to buyers.

Adjust pricing—Small service companies usually have lower operating costs than larger businesses, so they often price their services to customers for less. Contracts that create a backlog of business are of little value if the billing rates are so low the potential buyer couldn't make a profit. Raise prices to match the competition (who might be buyers for your business).

Transfer your knowledge—Accept the reality that you can be replaced. Sometimes our strengths become our weaknesses in that maybe you do know how best to serve your clients, but what happens if you're sick or overloaded with work? Get other people involved in your duties by teaching them how to do your job. This way when you, the owner, leave the business upon sale, the enterprise won't fall apart. This is the kind of assurance potential suitors want and need to have.

Pump up your marketing and exposure strategy—Today, many people think they can slap a website together and the world will come calling. In fact, websites do attract inquiries and they facilitate administrative functions. Yet they have zero value if you don't promote them. Advertise web sites in newspapers, magazines, on your letterhead and business cards, or any other place your audience might notice to help drive more business to the site and, ultimately, to increase your revenues.

Reduce employee turnover—If your business centers around the services you or your employees perform for clients, make sure those employees—the ones you've spent lots of time training—stick around by:

- Instituting programs that encourage them to stay, such as retirement with long-term vesting
- Compensating people well and giving them bonuses
- Creating a culture that is inviting and makes people bang down the door to come to work
- Treating employees like entrepreneurs

All of these steps will encourage a low turnover rate, making your business more profitable and stable—which is appealing to potential buyers.

Document and copyright your work—Training employees can be complex and time-consuming. It usually helps to have some sort of outline. Turn that information—which is how your business is run—into a manual so a buyer can take over with ease. Now you'll have something tangible when offering to sell the business. This sort of documentation of how your business runs is the way franchises begin. Franchisers are masters at documented processes, but everyone, even Mom and Pop shops, can and should do this.

Be prepared to defend—It's easy to copy some businesses. If the heart of your service business is "intellectual capital," then protect it. To prove you were there first, start by documenting who, what, where, when and how. Use service marks and trademarks. Copyright your materials. All of these steps are necessary if you ever need to defend your stake. By doing so, you also will be able to better assess and value your enterprise for potential sale or just to improve the way you run the business.

Take these steps to reveal and improve the value of service businesses. Then you can approach the bargaining table with low uncertainty and legitimate, documented indicators of business value—especially for those intangibles.

Calculating Indicators of Value

Now that you have taken steps to reveal the hidden value in a service, direct your attention to calculating indicators of business value. Minor adjustments to the valuation variables used in value indicator formulas will produce a helpful overall result.

Risk/Price Multiple

Service businesses often replace tangible assets with services people provide. A common example of this occurs in advertising and marketing businesses where the inventory is comprised of "people." Unlike a building, people are not static assets and can leave unexpectedly. This increases the risk involved with a service business. Indicators of value should account for this added risk. By modifying the criteria used to calculate a risk/price multiple, this becomes possible. RPM category headings are modified to target specific areas of emphasis in a small service business. Criteria in each category are refined for the same reason and limited to three considered most important. The resulting calculation of category averages and RPM is designed for the service business. This will be used as a variable to build the multiple of excess earnings indicator of value.

Finance—"Profitability"

The trend of favorable financial performance is of utmost importance when analyzing a service business. Establishing with some degree of certainty that results will continue is paramount. Accurate and thorough documentation that provide you with the ability to define the following items is crucial.

- 3-5 year business results
- Profit ($$$, % of net revenue)
- Cash flow and free cash flow
- Category average

Control—"Ownership Transition"

This is one measure of risk that is not dependent on the business performance prior to a sale. How an ownership transition is designed to occur, and how it is executed after the sale, should be given consideration. Where a business is relationship-based, this is especially true. So, give careful thought to the transition plan and commitment of parties to see it through.

- Mutually beneficial negotiated plan
- Term of continued involvement by the current owner
- Defined, meaningful seller support
- Category average

Marketing—"Company Size"

It can be difficult to determine the size of a service company when there are few, if any, meaningful comparable sales for reference. You can, however, compare it to competitors. In the case of a franchise, this problem is usually resolved by comparing the franchised service business to others in the same franchise group. The results of this comparison can be especially revealing. Particularly, since the new owner is likely to continue the franchise agreement.

- Business reputation and branding
- Effectiveness of advertising, publications and networking
- Number of account executives, clients and prospects
- Category average

Sales—"Relationships"

This might be the most important element of a service business because it is often no better than its relationships with others. If the new owner takes over and key account executives or clients depart, it can have a significantly unfavorable impact on revenue. Check the turnover rate to measure how effective current AE training and support programs are. If the rate of turnover is more than 50 percent, there is reason to be concerned. Additionally, if one person produces more than 50 percent of the total revenue, there is significant risk.

- Relationships of account executives with clients
- Account executive and client turnover rate
- Key person or client impact potential
- Category average

Production—"Operations"

If a service business is only as good as the people it attracts then there must be a robust and effective recruiting program. Examine this carefully. It's not enough to hire people, either. They must be properly trained to become productive and training should continue to ensure they stay that way. One effective solution to accomplish this is by having account executives work as teammates. It improves customer service and reduces risk to ownership if one decides to leave.

- Account executive recruiting, client/customer prospecting
- Account executive training, resources and support
- Use of teamwork among account executives/resource staff

Service—"Service Mix"

Providing quality service is the lifeblood of any service business. Look closely at the type of services offered to determine compatibility and synergy. More of these improve business results.

- Number of services available and cross promotion effectiveness
- Repeat vs. new business
- Industries, specialties, market niches served

It is readily apparent that more emphasis is placed on the account executives and clients because they are so important to continuing business operations. Also, considerable attention must be given to the quality of the ownership transition. In a service business, a new owner nearly always needs mentoring from the existing business owner. This can occur over a period of from 30 days to two years and is a very important consideration. Mentoring new owners ensures they succeed (so they are more likely to pay the asking price) and ensures sellers get paid if they finance a portion of the purchase price, which they often do.

Criteria used for each category can be customized further to suit specific businesses. For example, in the case of a franchise company, one might add "performance ranking within the franchise network" to Finance—"Profitability." To avoid watering-down the criteria, however, try to limit the number within each category to three. As before, use values of 1-5 to calculate the average of each category and the overall risk/price multiple.

Financing

Financing for a service business is more difficult to secure because account executives cannot be used as collateral for a loan. In some cases, client contracts might be considered, but generally only if they are assignable and the company is still in a position to service the clients in the event of a foreclosure. Additionally, the lower capital outlays required to start a service business now limits its ability to secure long-term financing. So, the most important other change in variables used to develop indicators of a service business's value is the term of financing. It will be shorter—generally, two, three, four or five years but seldom more. This may significantly reduce value indicated by levering the cash flow into equity and debt, when compared to a business with many tangible assets. This, however, is the price paid for the low-cost entry of a service business.

Capitalization Rate

The third valuation variable that may be adjusted to fit the service business profile is the capitalization rate used. Recall, a reasonable range of rates for small businesses might be the current prime lending rate times two, two and one-half, or even three, depending on risk. Favoring a higher rate will indicate the service business has greater risk. Keep in mind the value of comparable sales, if available, to confirm findings. These might be especially helpful if the property is a franchise.

Run the Numbers

This is a fitting parting thought for the *Business Valuation Bluebook*. It is also how one begins to understand and use indicators of business value. Running the numbers is the first thing to do when discovering a business opportunity. It is the last thing to do before buying it, something to be done throughout one's term of management and ownership, and just before inking the deal to sell it. If you are doing it correctly, you'll run the numbers forward, backward, and forward again to make sure they don't lie—because the numbers of a business are its story to be told. Looking deeply and learning to speak the language of indicators of value is how you read the book of a business. You may be first to discover a bestseller!

Appendix A
Shortcuts!

For those who want results without the research.

The fastest way to learn about indicators of value for small businesses and how to determine what they are worth is by learning the essentials and the vocabulary. This appendix is for those who want quick results with little research. If you catch on fast, this may be all you'll need. If you want to know more, the rest of the *Business Valuation Bluebook* is here to accommodate you.

Rules of Thumb

Working with small business is like exploring for gold in the Yukon Territories. There are few rules, no single formula to define value and no single value that works for everyone. The secret is finding a value that works for you. In that search, these rules of thumb almost always apply.

1) **Negotiate from Strength.** Weak arguments put you on the defense. Indicators of business value allow you to answer questions with confidence and play offense by asking penetrating questions.

2) **The Best Logic Often Wins.** Well-constructed positions usually prevail in negotiations. Sellers use them to support their position. Buyers do, too. He who uses them best enjoys a real win-win transaction...he wins regardless of the outcome.

3) **Results Matter.** Business earnings *must* provide for management compensation, pay a return on equity and retire acquisition debt. These are the results that matter to buyers who will verify them before they buy.

4) **Goodwill Is for Real.** The IRS says goodwill is the value of a business less the value of tangibles. Indicators of value e able you to calculate the former so it is easy to calculate the latter. In reality the question may not be if you have goodwill or not. The question is, "Do you know how to sell it by making the intangibles tangible?"

5) **Plan Ahead.** Smart sellers plan their exit a year before the business achieves its peak. Buyers witnessing the trend are encouraged and pay a premium.

6) **Make Your Money When You Buy.** Buy at the bottom when the business is a bargain. Collect your profit when you sell.

7) **Fortunes Are Made by Breaking with Tradition.** Chasing profits with the pack often insures you'll do no better than the rest. Leave the mainstream; follow a different path few are willing to take; be first to claim and keep profit from new sources of revenue.

8) **Cash Flow, Cash Flow, Cash Flow.** Cash flow is to a small business what location is to investment real estate. Businesses that have it sell for the highest price in the shortest time with the least effort.

Key Concepts

Several ideas are common to the practice of developing indicators of value for a small business. Here is a quick description of each.

Source of Business Value: A business includes income, assets and a marketing opportunity. Say the phrase "income, assets and a marketing opportunity" when asked what your business includes. Ask what you get from a business when buying. In each case, quantify the response received with indicators of business value.

Comparable Sales ("Comps"): Are they similar, recent or here? No two businesses operate exactly the same or produce the same results. Many comps are too old to be valid indicators of current value. The comps may serve different markets. One cannot be certain of the logic used to construct their business value (e.g., they could have been a bad investment).

Rules of Thumb: Shorthand indicators of value used to estimate business value. They are seldom complete, accurate, and definitive, and can be costly if relied upon excessively.

Indicators of Value: Indicators of value use intrinsic qualities of a business (cash flow, service mix, marketing power, etc.) and extrinsic factors (marketplace, location, competitiveness) to estimate value. Calculate them. They will do no less than save you time and make you money. They work.

Sources of Information: History is the best predictor of the future. Get and use historical results. Start with a business's trailing twelve months' earnings (TTE). Three to five years of financial records reveal trends that affect value.

Proforma Forecast: A proforma forecast means "operating as if" certain conditions come true. The only thing right about a proforma forecast is it is guaranteed to be wrong. If relying on a proforma forecast, make alternate forecasts and plans. You'll need them.

Indicators of Value: No single value is absolute. Develop several and home in on a range of values. Use the market, cost and income indicators of value to get the broadest perspective and more reliable results. That promotes confidence.

Valuation Variables: To identify business value, accurate valuation variables are required. Here's a list.

Earnings Reconstruction (ERCON)

An Earnings Reconstruction (ERCON) identifies the difference between net profit (taxable income) and cash flow (what the owner actually keeps). The simplest reconstruction is EBIT (Earnings Before Interest and Taxes). EBITDA is next and includes EBIT plus Depreciation and Amortization expenses. Add operating owner's salary, personal benefits (perks) paid by the business as expenses, and deduct potential increased expenses due to an ownership change to calculate CASH FLOW, the mother of all valuation variables.

EARNINGS RECONSTRUCTION
BELL-Quest, Ltd.

Revenue	$ 608,951
Cost of Goods	<390,190>
Gross Profit	$ 218,761
Expenses	<$ 189,501>
Net Profit	$ 29,260
Interest	$ 4,533
Taxes	----
EBIT	$ 33,793
Depreciation	4,809
Amortization	1,668
EBITDA	$ 40,270
Owner's Salary	18,000
Non-Recurring Expenses	502
Net Adjustments to EBITDA	$ 18,502
CASH FLOW	$ 58,772

Free Cash Flow

Cash flow less management compensation.

Equity Set-Aside

Holding out some of the free cash flow to be used as a return on equity. How much? Try using a percent that is equal to the percent of down payment a buyer would be expected to contribute toward the purchase of the business.

FMV Tangibles

The Fair Market Value (FMV) of tangible assets is the amount one could reasonably expect to pay for an asset. Or it is the value or cost to replace an asset with another of like-kind.

Safe Rate of Return

A safe rate of return is the interest rate one could reasonably expect to receive from a secure investment. When held to maturity, highly rated long-term corporate or municipal bonds are examples of investments that provide safe rates of return. Often 1 percent less than the prime rate.

Capitalization Rate

This term, also known as cap rate, refers to the rate at which a stream of future payments converts into a present value. It is expressed as a rate, like interest. For example, an investment capable of producing $1,000 of income capitalized at 10 percent, indicates a present value of $10,000. Expressed mathematically that is:

$$\frac{\$1{,}000 \text{ (Income)}}{10\% \text{ (Cap Rate)} \times \$10{,}000 \text{ (Value)}}$$

For small businesses the cap rate can be a combination of a base rate (prime interest rate) plus a risk premium. This can be any amount ranging from 50 percent of prime times 2 or more up to a total rate of 12 percent over prime. It is a matter of personal preference, however, because cash flows of small businesses, markets, industries and investor criteria always differ. Ex. 5.5% x 2 = 11% etc.

Business RPM

A risk/price multiple is often called a "pricing multiple." The RPM measures both risk and indications of value from intrinsic *and* extrinsic considerations. A subjective value scale to use when determining a business's risk/price multiple.

5 = MINIMAL RISK
Excellent control, many opportunities, profitable.

4 = LOW RISK
Good control over growth and equity. Secure.

3 = ACCEPTABLE RISK
Market and management forces can prevail.

2 = RISKY
Small margins for error, but recovery is possible.

1 = HIGH RISK
Loss of equity likely. Crisis management prevails.

0 = MAXIMUM RISK
Business is out of control. Failure is likely.

To create an RPM, divide the business into seven categories: Finance, Control, Marketing, Sales, Production, Service and Intellectual Capital. For a service business, change these categories to Profitability, Ownership Transition, Market Size, Relationships, Operations and Service Mix. Evaluate each with a score of 5 – 0. The average of these category scores is the risk price multiple.

Financing

Nearly all businesses involve financing. Certain methods to indicate value lever cash flow into equity and debt. Financing variables are needed and include interest rates, loan terms, debt coverage and loan-to-value ratios.

Indicator of Value—Capitalize the Income

A "market" indicator of value using a capitalization rate that might apply to business investments similar in size, type and markets. The basic method requires three variables: income, cap rate and value. Any two can be used to calculate the third with the formula appearing below.

CAPITALIZATING INCOME
BELL-Quest, Ltd.

$$\frac{\$13,107 \ (I)}{13.75\% \ (R)} = \$95,324$$
(Value without Real Estate)

Indicator of Value—A Multiple of Excess Earnings

An "asset-based" indicator of value because this formula adds costs to acquire tangible and intangible property to indicate value. Helps answer the question *What's my goodwill worth?* This technique works best with companies holding many tangibles and has limited benefit with service-type companies where tangibles are limited.

MULTIPLE OF EXCESS EARNINGS
BELL-Quest, Ltd.

VARIABLES

Free Cash Flow	$	13,107
Safe Rate of Return		4.5%
Tangible Assets	$	60,000
RPM		2.31
Business Free Cash Flow	$	13,107
Tangible Assets	$	60,000
Safe Rate of Return		4.5%
Return on Tangible Assets		<2,700>
Business Excess Earnings	$	10,047
Risk/Price Multiple		2.06
Value of Excess Earnings	$	20,697
Value of Tangible Assets		60,000
ESTIMATED BUSINESS VALUE	$	88,697

Indicator of Value–Levering Cash Flow

The "income approach" or gold standard of indicators of value because it addresses a buyer's ability to pay debt and a return on equity from cash flow.

LEVERING CASH FLOW
BELL-Quest, Ltd.
(Seller Financing)

VARIABLES:

Free Cash Flow	$	13,107
Equity Set-Aside @ 25%	$	3,277
Tangible Assets	$	60,000
Capitalization Rate		16.5%

Step 1: Calculate Monthly Payments For Debt

Annual Debt Service	$	9,830.25
(÷) Payments per period		(÷) 12
Monthly Payments	$	819.19

Step 2: Determine Amount of Financing

Interest Rate		5.5%
Loan Term		7
Monthly Payment	$	819.19
Balance on Due Date		0
Serviceable Debt		$ 57,006.78

Step 3: Determine Business Value

Affordable Loan Balance	$ 57,006.78
(+) Equity ($3,277/13.75%)	$ 23,469.09
BUSINESS VALUE	$ 80,475.88

Range of Results

Calculate this to examine the overall accuracy of the indicators of value.

CALCULATED VALUES BELL-Quest, Ltd. Without Real Estate	
Capitalizing Income	$ 95,324
Multiple of Excess Earnings	$ 88,697
Levering Cash Flow (Seller Financed)	$ 80,476

Using measures of central tendency the business market value is estimated to be $88,166 (mean) or $87,900 (median).

RANGE ANALYSIS BELL-Quest, Ltd. To Determine Market Value	
Mean Value	$ 88,166
Range	$ 14,848
Median of Range	$ 7,424
Low Value in the Range	$ 80,476
Median Value	$ 87,900

Indication of Value from Assets

Add FMV tangibles to the annual salary of a full-time operating owner.

Estimate Wholesale Value of Inventory from Retail Value

Divide the retail value by 1.00 plus the percent of markup. The answer is the wholesale value.

How to Defeat an Asking Price Using Income

Variables needed are the asking price, an estimate of financing required, business cash flow and reasonable management compensation. Simply calculate the payments required for financing. Subtract the annual debt service from the cash flow. Compare what remains to the management compensation. If it is more, the price has merit. If what remains is less, ask the seller if he would be willing to work for that amount to run the business.

How to Defeat an Asking Price Using Goodwill

Variables needed are the asking price, FMV tangibles and management compensation. Subtract the FMV tangibles from the asking price to calculate goodwill. Compare this to annual management compensation. If it is less, the asking price may have merit. If it is more, it could be too high. Ownership of both a business and the real estate it occupies is common among small business entrepreneurs. This arrangement often results in a special situation when it is time to plan an exit strategy. In essence, both properties may be available when it is time to sell out. Ownership frequently attempts to sell them as a package deal for one price. Valuable marketing and income benefits might be realized, however, by offering these properties as separate investments.

Finance: "Don't put long-term loans on short-term assets."

Skimming: "It's the part of the purchase price you get before you sell."

Profits: "You can increase revenue or reduce costs, but you cannot save yourself into prosperity."

Growth: "Raise the number of units sold or raise the price...or both."

Analysis: "You don't need a million-dollar solution for a thousand-dollar problem."

Risk: "Calculate risk to err on the side of caution."

Service: "It's always cheaper and easier to keep customers than find new ones."

Win-Win: "The best kind of 'win-win' is when you win either way."

Experience: "Good judgment comes from experience. Experience comes from bad judgment."

Investing: "You make your money when you buy."

Ownership: "Freedom of choice."

Action: "It's easier to get forgiveness than permission."

Strategy: "Do what everyone else does and do it better, or do something others don't do at all."

Opportunity: "The opportunity of a lifetime comes along every 45 days."

Strength: "What makes you good can make you bad."

Focus: "The problem with casting a wide net is it gets full of holes."

Loyalty: "Dance with them that brung you."

Quality: "Quality costs when you don't have it."

Planning: "Nolo supre prendre!" (No surprises!)

Appendix B
General Terms and Features
of Acquisitions

This material is for general information purposes only. Laws governing small business acquisitions and dispositions change periodically. State laws affecting these issues vary widely. This material is not to be considered as legal, accounting, or tax advice. Readers are strongly advised to speak with their respective legal, accounting, or tax consultants before attempting to employ any of the information or concepts stated in this appendix.

ACQUISITION AGREEMENT When the buyer and seller reach an agreement to transfer a business, by the basic structure of this transaction (terms and conditions), a written acquisition agreement should be prepared. Generally buyers prepare the initial acquisition agreement since it is they who are advancing an offer.

Many acquisition agreements are prepared on a standard form. These can be effective, provided they meet all the needs of the parties involved. Many do not. Most, however, will share the same elements, which are listed here.

- Identity of assets or stock to be sold, the price and terms, and the mechanics or rules governing the transaction.

- Other conditions of the agreement including, but not limited to, amount of earnest money or deposit delivered with the acquisition agreement, financing, provisions for a covenant not to compete, training to be provided by the seller, earnout provisions, etc.

- Representations and warranties of the seller, e.g., when real estate is included, the seller may warrant title to the property is good and marketable.

- Representations and warranties of the buyer.

- Covenants pending a closing.

- Conditions precedent to a closing.

- Provisions of the closing or termination of the agreement, e.g., setting the time and place of closing, form of funds to be brought to the closing, etc. Also may include a penalty for failure to close when all other conditions of the agreement have been satisfied—often forfeiture of a percentage of the sales price, which may be taken from the deposit.

- Indemnifications of the parties involved—buyer to seller, seller to buyer, both to lender, their professional representatives, etc.

- Provision of payment for fees, expenses and other miscellaneous matters.

ACQUISITION OF ASSETS VERSUS STOCK - Many small businesses are closely held. This means they have a small number of owners or are family owned. They may be incorporated, too.

When acquiring a business that has been incorporated, most buyers prefer to acquire the assets from the corporation or partnership instead of the stock in the legal entity. This occurs because the company, not its stockholders, owns the business assets. The stockholders own stock in the company. Here are two important reasons.

When acquiring assets, buyers establish a new value for the depreciable tangible and intangible assets being purchased. It may be larger than the property's basis under current ownership. The new, greater value increases the amount of depreciation and amortization that may be taken by a buyer. This value often compares favorably to the remaining tax benefit available to the corporation that owns the assets.

There may be certain liabilities that accompany ownership of a corporation. These may be outstanding financial obligations or existing and potential liabilities created by lawsuits. These can pass to a buyer as the new owner of company stock.

To avoid unintended assumption of liabilities and to establish a new basis for depreciation of assets, buyers often elect to buy business assets rather than outstanding stock.

ALLOCATION OF PRICE - The sale of a business involves the sale of tangible and intangible assets. The total of all property acquired is the purchase price. The purpose of the allocation is to establish a new basis for depreciation and amortization based on the fair market value of the property involved.

As a condition precedent to closing, a value must be placed on each asset acquired. Assets are tangible or intangible. Both parties must agree to the allocation, which can have varying tax consequences for each. Allocation should be done by the parties' tax consultants or other qualified professional representatives. The Internal Revenue Service has the authority to review allocations it considers unreasonable.

APPRAISAL - As a condition precedent to a closing, a property appraisal is often requested to confirm value. A buyer, seller, or lender providing financing to the buyer acquiring property may require this. Payment for the appraisal may be negotiated between the parties. In those cases where a business acquisition is contemplated, business valuation skill on the part of the buyer or lender will be most helpful. The supply of qualified business appraisers is small to nonexistent in rural areas.

APPROVALS - Prior to closing, many approvals may be needed. These are conditions precedent to a closing. Typical approvals needed for most acquisitions are:

- Approval of licensing or franchising authorities
- Approval of lender for financing
- Approval of buyers' or their professional representatives' review of financials and all other aspects of the business operation and operating agreements

- Approval of the buyer's financial qualifications where seller financing is involved
- Approval of stockholders when necessary

As a general rule, it is best to secure as many approvals as possible prior to the closing. This prevents last-minute changes that can often occur.

ASSUMPTION OF DEBT - Many times a business sold will have existing debt. Buyers may elect to assume the debt and, if so, should state the terms and conditions under which this may occur. Various questions should be considered. If debt assumption is to be renegotiated, when is this to be completed? Will the seller's guarantee be released or not? Is the buyer given permission to discuss the outstanding debt with the appropriate creditors?

In other instances, the buyer may want to acquire a business free and clear of debts, liens, and encumbrances of any kind. Normally this is more to a buyer's liking and is especially preferred when a lender is providing acquisition financing. In such cases the agreement will discuss the nature, size, and terms of outstanding business debts together with a condition that they will be paid in full at closing.

ASSUMPTION OF AGREEMENTS - A condition that provides for a buyer's assumption of agreements usually refers to a franchise agreement. It may also include special arrangements with business vendors or professionals representing the business whose involvement is to be continued. These would be noted in the acquisition agreement.

BILL OF SALE - A bill of sale is evidence a transfer of personal property has occurred. Because real estate is not included in the sale of many businesses, a bill of sales is a common form of conveyance. Where real estate is included, conveyance is by way of a deed.

BULK SALES LAW - Many states have a bulk sales law. This is commonly applied to transactions where an inventory for resale is included in the sale. The bulk sales provisions require that notification be given to a business's creditors prior to the sale of property or sale of a business where credit has been extended. Under a bulk sales law the creditor can make claims for payment prior to the closing.

The intended result of a bulk sales law is to draw a line between debts of the buyer and debts of the seller. Creditors are paid from the rightful debtor, and a business is conveyed without debts except those a buyer assumes and agrees to pay. In some states a Uniform Commercial Code provides for payment of creditors out of sales proceeds.

A problem with the bulk sales law occurs among buyers and sellers who do not want to notify creditors of a sale, and forfeit confidentiality. This can be of particular concern to a seller when a closing remains in doubt. Buyers, as the new owners of the business, do not want outstanding debts to surface as claims against them. Even when the buyer is not responsible for payment, creditors have been known to refuse delivery of additional merchandise until outstanding claims are paid by prior ownership or anyone else.

As a compromise, some buyers and sellers agree to circumvent the bulk sales provisions. The seller gives the buyer a list of outstanding business debts as of the closing, agreeing to pay them from closing proceeds furnished by the buyer. Thereafter, the seller may be willing to escrow additional closing proceeds for a short time. These can be used to pay off other undisclosed debts if any are discovered. If none exist, escrowed funds are released to the seller. As an additional provision, the seller may agree to indemnify and hold the buyer harmless for any liabilities incurred from creditor claims that originated prior to the closing.

COVENANTS PENDING A CLOSING - These are items that restrict or obligate buyer and seller to take prior to the closing, or the covenant may forbid taking certain actions. An example is restricting the release of information to parties to the transaction and their professional representatives. Other covenants might require the sellers to continue normal business operations, conducting no unusual activities such as a going-out-of-business sale; to keep the negotiations strictly confidential; to keep the business property well maintained and insured; and to make timely payment of all taxes and financial obligations prior to closing.

COVENANT NOT TO COMPETE - A covenant not to compete—a non-competition agreement—is generally given from a seller to a buyer. It is important when the seller possesses technical knowledge about the business being purchased that could be used by a competitor to attract the market share of the business. The result would be a reduction of revenue and performance created by the seller's actions after a closing.

Most covenants not to compete include four key provisions: a term, a geographic reference, the type of activity not permitted, and a value. There may be other conditions as well, including remedies for violation of the covenant.

CONDITIONS PRECEDENT TO CLOSING -Actions a buyer or seller must, or must not, do to accomplish an activity are conditions precedent to a closing. For example, buyers or their professional representatives must review and approve the business financials within ten business days from the date the acquisition agreement is fully executed.

Here is a partial list of the topics that might be included as a condition, which is to be performed or subject to review and approval. Note the list is by no means complete and could include many other conditions that might pertain to a unique buyer or business situation.

- Financing commitment
- Appraisal of property
- Financial statements review
- Business operations review
- Due diligence

- Training or training plan for buyer
- Credit, financial and qualifications of buyer
- Business, franchise and professional service agreements
- Review of customer and vendor lists
- Approvals from licensing and regulatory authorities
- Completed physical inventory and approval
- Review of all tangibles and intangibles
- Review of debt and liabilities assumed
- Bulk sales compliance
- Sales tax treatment of inventory purchased
- Certificate of good standing and all other documentation

EARNEST MONEY - When arranging transactions to sell and buy businesses and/or real estate, the ability to keep a transaction from falling apart is often related to the amount of earnest money placed on deposit by a buyer. When a substantial earnest money deposit is made, the buyer is more committed to perform. In such instances a seller also is more willing to take the buyer seriously. A promissory note or a dollar bill clipped to an offer simply will not do.

Receipt and use of earnest money is a negotiable issue. It may be delivered in one or more installments. These can begin at the first execution date of the acquisition agreement and continue as conditions are completed in an orderly sequence. Earnest money may be refundable if certain conditions precedent to a closing remain unfulfilled by closing or a certain date stated earlier. Certain expenses, such as appraisal fees, may be deducted from the earnest money. In other instances, where conditions are fully executed, the earnest money is credited to the purchase price of the property.

EARNOUTS - An earnout is a form of payment buyers offer sellers where there is uncertainty about the future performance of a business. To implement an earnout strategy, the buyer will acquire the business and agree to pay additional premiums to the seller based on business results received. A simple form of earnout would be where the seller receives a small percentage of the increase in business revenue. If the results improve, the selling party is rewarded. If results decline, no additional payment is made.

Earnouts are a good way to test a seller's confidence in the future of a business. Earnout provisions keep a seller committed to working for the continued success of the enterprise (i.e., there is a direct financial incentive for this support).

EXPIRATION OF OFFERS - An expiration of offer occurs when the acquisition agreement includes a date by which a response from the seller is required. If none is received, the offer is withdrawn. Buyers often place expiration dates in acquisition offers to encourage a timely response from sellers; if no response is received, the buyer moves on. Sometimes an expiration date is used to pressure a seller into quick acceptance. This tactic is unhelpful because it usually results in a seller's avoidance of the offer entirely, or sellers attach additional provisions that have a nullifying effect on the expiration date. The seller's response may also be accompanied by an equally short deadline for the buyer's acceptance of added provisions.

An expiration of offer that provides a seller with a reasonable amount of time to consider the proposition is an acceptable approach. Such an expiration should be included to prevent sellers from holding the offer indefinitely and attempting to find other offers that are better. Also, a reasonable expiration date helps ensure the buyer's proposal is not accepted at a later time after the buyer has made an investment elsewhere.

FINANCING - Since most buyers of businesses want to use investment leverage in acquisitions, a condition providing them with a chance to secure a financing commitment is frequently included in an acquisition agreement.

Buyers often state very specific terms of financing requested. Sellers counter by adjusting them to reflect outside limits. For example, a seller might modify the buyer's statement of terms that seek financing at 9 percent annual interest rate to financing that does not exceed 10 percent. The difference is the buyer could use a commitment of financing at 8.5 percent as a device to void the contract *for any other reason*. The seller's approach would eliminate this loophole.

In general, when securing financing is a condition precedent to closing, the terms stated are amount, interest rate, loan term, method of payment, collateral, and personal guarantees involved.

FUTURE BUSINESS ASSURANCES - Occasionally buyers ask sellers to state that they know of no events occurring or about to occur that could negatively affect business performance. This is not an unreasonable condition. Sellers respond, however, by stating that they are delivering the business "as is" and no warranties for future performance are made or implied.

This is an important issue since the earnings reconstruction used in a business valuation process is designed to reveal the differences between taxable income and cash flow. Earnings reconstructions are not a tool to forecast the future. An earnings reconstruction is an indication of what has been and is based entirely on trailing earnings. For this reason, sellers creating a value range based on next year's cash flow are well advised to keep their cash flow forecasts to themselves. If desired, buyers should construct these with the help of their professional representatives.

More importantly, when a final or year-end financial statement is to be received between a letter of intent or acquisition agreement and closing, it is unwise to link approval of the business's financial condition to receipt of these documents. They could reveal a dramatic downturn in business. It is better to state the business results should reflect no change in business revenue, or should include improvements that can be defined.

GOOD STANDING OF CORPORATION - States require corporations to pay what is commonly called a "franchise tax." The state gives its permission for you to operate your business. A certificate of good standing accompanies the entity's ability to legally operate and conduct lawful business in the state. This certificate is a statement from regulatory authorities to indicate a corporation is in compliance, taxes are paid, and the entity is in "good standing." This certificate is often requested as a condition precedent to a closing. It ensures the corporation selling the assets has the authority to act.

INDEMNIFICATION - This is a condition whereby the parties to an agreement each agree to compensate the other for damages or losses that may occur. In an acquisition agreement, the sellers would indemnify buyers against any losses that might occur as a result of debts not assumed by the buyer and unpaid by the seller.

How might this occur? Suppose a liquor store changes hands July 1, and the seller fails to pay an outstanding invoice for beer delivered. The new owner places an order for more stock to be received by July 3. The vendor refuses to deliver until the outstanding invoice is paid. The loss of sales can be substantial and, under certain conditions, the buyer might have a claim.

Pending litigation and undisclosed liabilities are common reasons a seller will indemnify a buyer. Brokers guiding a business transaction often state in the acquisition agreement that they have made no representations. They further state that execution of the agreement by the parties is their agreement to indemnify the broker against consequences of the transaction.

INSPECTIONS - Inspections may be a condition precedent to closing. Approvals often accompany the inspections as well as a date by which approval is to be received. Handled in this way, inspections are gradually removed and pose no roadblock to closing.

Inspections may include:

- Business financials
- Agreements such as leases, franchises, employment contracts, professional service agreements, etc.

- Business property, including real estate and improvements, furnishings, fixtures and equipment
- Operating procedures

INTANGIBLES - Property that contributes to business performance but cannot be touched or felt is intangible property. Covenants not to compete, goodwill, customer lists and a franchise are common forms of intangible assets. The acquisition agreement should state the intangibles acquired together with those intangibles' allocated values.

INVENTORY - Acquisition agreements for the purchase of a retail business will state, as a condition precedent to closing, the inventory must be counted just prior to closing. This provision will often name the service that will perform the inventory and govern the process. Both buyer and seller should be present at the inventory to approve of the process. Buyers may want to exclude certain types of inventory that appear damaged or dated.

When taking an inventory for most small businesses, the easiest method to use involves categorizing all merchandise by markup. For example, all merchandise in one category is marked up 30 percent, items in another category are marked up 40 percent, and the rest is marked up 20 percent. Merchandise is counted at its retail value. Divide the total by 1.00 plus the percent of markup to identify actual cost of the merchandise. This is a simple and generally acceptable way to determine the value of inventory that will be included with the business at the closing, which should follow immediately after the inventory.

When offered for sale, a business may be priced plus or including inventory at seller's cost. The difference can be meaningful when attempting to attract a buyer. One price is much lower but more uncertain; the other is higher but instills more confidence in the buyer. Using the seller's cost, if the inventory at closing is less than the amount stated to be present in the acquisition agreement, the price is adjusted accordingly. If the amount of inventory is greater, the buyer may pay the added amount, issue a credit to the seller for merchandise in the future, or if applicable, add the additional amount to seller financing.

LETTER OF INTENT - A letter of intent may be used as a precedent to an acquisition agreement. A buyer prepares a letter of intent, signs it and delivers it to the seller, who signs it too. The letter of intent is executed prior to a formal acquisition agreement.

Letters of intent are helpful when there is a need to commit a basic agreement between buyer and seller to writing. This prevents future misunderstanding and helps avoid renegotiation. Also, a letter of intent conveys a moral commitment between the parties. To the extent that business people keep their word, a letter of intent is helpful to move a transaction along. Letters of intent generally have several common elements:

- A statement of whether the letter of intent is binding or not

- A statement of whether a formal acquisition agreement will be prepared, in which case the letter of intent is subject to that document's execution

- The form of the transaction: Is it an asset purchase, the purchase of a business with or without real estate, or a purchase of company stock?

- The price and terms

- Significant provisions, covenants and conditions precedent to execution of the acquisition agreement and or a closing

For obvious reasons, letters of intent also are helpful when the time until an actual acquisition agreement is executed will be lengthy.

LIMITATION OF LIABILITY - One way entrepreneurs attempt to reduce exposure created by indemnifications is to establish an upper limit on their liability. This may be a reasonable request, provided the limit is established at an appropriate level. Some feel the liability should not exceed the value of property conveyed. Others feel the limit should be tied to historical limits, if they exist. In any case, when limitations on liability are introduced, the other party is given a reason for concern.

Also, when indemnity is given to prevent liability, parties attempt to secure joint and several liabilities. Normally this occurs when more than one individual is liable for an obligation. When used, all individuals are each liable for the entire obligation —not on their prorated share of the obligation. Thus, collection is easier because it is presumed certain members of a group who are jointly and severally liable will encourage full payment from the entire group.

MISREPRESENTATION - Buyers and sellers make statements about themselves and their businesses to each other. When it is discovered—usually by a due diligence or background check—that something has been omitted that should not have been, a misrepresentation may have occurred.

The severity of misrepresentations is often determined by the intent or non-intent to omit information, and whether or not it is material to the terms and conditions of the acquisition agreement. Where a misrepresentation is intentional and material, a buyer's typical recourse is to walk away from the transaction. If the transaction has already occurred, a buyer's recourse may include legal remedies.

PHYSICAL CONDITION OF FIXED ASSETS - As a condition precedent to closing, a buyer may want assurances that all property purchased is in good working condition. Inspections are typical for real estate, and this may require wording to allow professional inspectors access to the property for the purpose of making specific inspections. Inspections are often at the buyer's expense. A provision may be inserted into the agreement to resolve any dispute arising from assets found to be in poor condition.

REPRESENTATIONS - These are statements a seller usually makes to a buyer that indicate the condition of a business being acquired.

They often refer to other statements—the financials of the business—and are subject to verification. Representations are normally tied to a date that has already passed. Changes after that date are the subject of additional disclosures.

RIGHT OF RECISION - Acquisition agreements for a small business may include a right of recision for the buyer. This means that within a specified period of time, usually determined by state statutes, the buyer may elect to cancel the agreement. The term in which a right of recision may be exercised is usually short, 24 to 48 hours.

SALES TAXES - When the form of acquisition is an asset purchase, it may be necessary to state certain provisions to describe the purchase of inventory. This can be necessary because if improperly done, or omitted, a buyer purchasing inventory could be liable for payment of sales taxes on the entire amount purchased. This can be substantial. Because sales taxes are affected by state and local regulations, the buyer should carefully investigate sales tax rules with the assistance of local authorities.

TANGIBLES - Tangibles are the property being conveyed that has physical form and substance. This includes real property but, more specifically, refers to personal property such as business furnishings, fixtures, equipment, leasehold improvements, and inventory. The acquisition agreement should allocate a reasonable value to each tangible asset conveyed in the transaction. This value normally becomes the basis used to calculate the amount of depreciation a buyer will receive in the future, and the amount of gain a seller will receive from the sale.

TRAINING - Another provision of the acquisition agreement requires the seller to train the buyer in all aspects of business operations. When used, the amount and term of training should be specified. Also, sellers often receive compensation for their involvement.

The acquisition agreement should indicate if this compensation is to be considered as income or as part of the price paid for the business.

Appendix C
Business Valuation Forms

Shortcut to Estimate Business Cash Flow
Earnings Reconstruction Formula
Calculating Business RPM Pricing Multiple
Formulas to Challenge and Reduce Value

- Capitalization Method

- Excess Earnings Method

- Leveraged Cash Flow Method (Seller Financing)

- Leveraged Cash Flow Method (Bank Financing)

Due Diligence Checklists

- Finance

- Control

- Marketing

- Sales

- Production

- Service

Shortcut to Estimate Cash Flow

This technique is used to develop a rough estimate of a business cash flow with limited information. It works well because sellers do not feel answers to questions asked will be too revealing. Knowing how to calculate cost of goods from revenue and a percent markup is the key. This technique is fully described in Chapter 4. To develop the estimate, the entrepreneur asks three questions and performs four simple steps listed below. Answers may be received by asking a seller during an initial meeting.

- "How much is the average revenue per month?"

- "What is the average markup on merchandise sold?"

- "On average, what are the cash expenses of the business, excluding owner's salary, each month?"

STEP 1: Calculate Cost of Goods

Revenue ÷ 1.00 + Percent of Markup = Cost of Goods

$50,000 ÷ 1.00 + .30 (130%) = $38,451.54

STEP 2: Calculate Business Gross Profit

Revenue – Cost of Goods = Gross Profit

$50,000 - $38,451.54 = $11,548.46

STEP 3: Calculate Estimate of Business Cash Flow

Gross Profit – Expenses = Cash Flow

$11,548.46 - $6,000 = $5,548.46

STEP 4: Estimate Annual Cash Flow

Monthly Cash Flow x Months Per Year = Annual Cash Flow

$5,548.46 x 12 = $66,581.52

Appendix C

SUBJECT PROPERTY: _____

DATE: _____

EARNINGS RECONSTRUCTION

Period: _____ **to** _____

Revenue		$_____
Cost of Goods	< $_____ >	
Gross Profit		$_____
Expenses	< $_____ >	
Net Profit		$_____
Interest	$_____	
Taxes	$_____	
EBIT (Earnings Before Interest & Taxes)	$_____	
Depreciation	$_____	
Amortization	$_____	
EBITDA (EBIT, plus Depreciation & Amortization)		$_____
Positive Adjustments		
Education		$_____
Employee Benefits		$_____
Entertainment	$_____	
Home Office	$_____	
Mortgage Interest	$_____	
Non-Recurring Expenses	$_____	
Payroll (Owners Plus/Minus Other)	$_____	
Transportation	$_____	
Travel	$_____	
_____	$_____	
_____	$_____	
Negative Adjustments		
_____	< $_____ >	
_____	< $_____ >	
_____	< $_____ >	
Net Adjustments		$_____

BUSINESS CASH FLOW $_____

SUBJECT PROPERTY: _____

DATE: _____

BUSINESS RPM (Pricing Multiple) CALCULATOR

Period: _____ to _____

FINANCE _____

Trailing Revenue _____

Revenue Momentum _____

Capital Structure _____

Leverage Opportunities _____

Earnings & Cash Flow _____

CONTROL _____

Employee Turnover Rate
& Cost (ETOR/ETOC) _____

Employee Compensation _____

Contingency Planning _____

Network Penetration _____

Potential Litigation _____

MARKETING _____

Well-Defined Marketing Plan _____

Branded Power _____

Market Differentiation _____

Market Segmentation _____

E-Commerce Activity _____

SALES _____

Type of Service or Product _____

Sales Process Fit _____

Sales Incentives Available _____

Sales Training Programs _____

Wired Distribution _____

PRODUCTION   _____

Emphasis on Quality   _____

Innovation   _____

Capacity Vs. Demand   _____

Obsolescence   _____

Inventory Management   _____

SERVICE   _____

Integrated Vision   _____

Employee Recognition   _____

Team Spirit   _____

Flexibility   _____

Open Communication   _____

INTELLECTUAL CAPITAL (Optional)   _____

Customer Satisfaction   _____

Employee Motivation   _____

Potential Synergies   _____

Key People   _____

Institutional Intelligence   _____

BUSINESS RPM (Pricing Multiple)   _____

SUBJECT PROPERTY: _____

DATE: _____

CAPITALIZATION METHOD OF VALUE

Period: _____ **to** _____

I (income) $_____

R (rate)   _____ %

V (value) $_____

$$\frac{I}{R \times V}$$

Note#1

- Income divided by Rate equals Value

- Income divided by Value equals Rate

- Rate times Value equals Income

Note #2 - To calculate business values when one is not given, select a capitalization rate. Use free cash flow as income.

To challenge a given business value, solve for rate. Compare this to investor expectations. Or, solve for income and compare it to the actual free cash flow available.

When differences between expected and actual rate/income exist, substitute the market rate expected for the rate offered and solve for the indicated business value.

SUBJECT PROPERTY: _____

DATE: _____

EXCESS EARNINGS METHOD OF VALUE

Period: _____ to _____

Variables

Free Cash Flow $_____   Safe Rate _____%

Tangible Assets $_____   RPM   _____

Business Free Cash Flow		$_____
Tangible Assets		$_____
(x) Safe Rate of Return		_____%
Return on Tangible Assets	$_____	< $_____ >
Business Excess Earnings		$_____
(x) RPM (Pricing Multiple)		_____
Value of Excess Earnings		$_____
(+) Value of Tangible Assets		$_____

ESTIMATED BUSINESS VALUE $_____

Excess Earnings Challenge

Business Value $_____

(-) Market Value of Tangible Assets   < $_____ >

Value of Excess Earnings $_____

Value of Excess Earnings $_____

(÷) Amount of Excess Earnings $_____

RPM (Pricing Multiple)   _____

Note#1 - Substitute actual RPM for indicated and recalculate value of excess earnings and business value.

SUBJECT PROPERTY: _____

DATE: _____

LEVERAGED CASH FLOW^{SF} METHOD OF VALUE

Period: _____ **to** _____

Variables:

Free Cash Flow $_____   RPM   _____

Tangible Assets $_____   Mgt. Comp. $_____

_____

STEP 1: Calculate Monthly Payments for Debt

Free Cash Flow $_____

($\div$) Payments per period (Annual = 12)   _____

Monthly Payment Amount $_____

STEP 2: Determine Amount of Financing

Interest Rate   _____%

Loan Term   _____

Monthly Payment $_____

Balance on Due Date $_____

Serviceable Debt $_____

STEP 3: Determine Business Value

Serviceable Debt (Financing) $_____

(+)Equity ("X" times Management Comp.) $_____

BUSINESS VALUE $_____

Note#1 - Substitute variables and terms of finance and recalculate for value. Compare against the asking price to challenge its accuracy.

Note#2 - The superscript "SF" in the title indicates this formula is generally used with seller financing where financing is secured from only one source.

SUBJECT PROPERTY: _____

DATE: _____

LEVERAGED CASH FLOW^{BF} METHOD OF VALUE
Period: _____ **to** _____

Variables:

Free Cash Flow	$_____	RPM	_____	
Tangible Assets	$_____	Mgt. Comp.	$____	
DCR	$_____	LTV	_____%	

STEP 1: Calculate Monthly Payments for Debt

Free Cash Flow	$_____
(÷) Payments per period (Annual = 12)	_____
Monthly Payment Amount	$_____

STEP 2: Determine Amount of Financing

	1st Mortgage	2nd Mortgage
Interest Rate	_____%	_____%
Loan Term	_____	_____
Monthly Payment	$_____	$_____
Balance on Due Date	$_____	$_____
Serviceable Debt	$_____	$_____

STEP 3: Determine Business Value

Combined Serviceable Debt (Financing)	$_____
(+)Equity ("X" times Management Comp.)	$_____
BUSINESS VALUE	$_____

Note#1 - Substitute variables and terms of finance and recalculate for value. Compare against the asking price to challenge its accuracy.

Note#2 - The superscript "BF" in the title indicates this formula is generally used with bank financing. This often results in more than one loan—the seller often takes a second.

SUBJECT PROPERTY: _____

DATE: _____

DUE DILIGENCE CHECKLISTS

(An asterisk "*" denotes key information needed)

Period: _____ **to** _____

FINANCE CHECKLIST

1. Contact Persons (name, address, phone, fax and e-mail of each)
___ Business principal*
___ General manager
___ In-house bookkeeper
___ Certified public accountant
___ Banking representative

2. Mortgages and Notes Payable
___ Principal balances*
___ Term of loan/interest rate/payment amount
___ Payoff date and penalties associated
___ Collateral pledges
___ Identity of persons signing and guaranteeing payment

3. Leases for Location and Equipment
___ Description of location or materials covered by the lease
___ Amount of lease payments due*
___ Payment schedules
___ Term of the lease and options to renew
___ Responsibilities (who pays for what)

4. Accounts Receivable/Payable
___ Amount of each*
___ Separate each into 30, 60, 90 and 0ver 90 days due
___ Historical record of changes in both
___ Ratio of accounts receivable to accounts payable over time*
___ Collection procedures
___ Cash or accrual method of accounting used
___ Estimate of revenue from work under contract but not performed*
___ Estimate of work to be performed eventually but not under contract

5. Financial Statements
___ Balance sheets for three to five years*
___ P&L statements for three to five years*
___ Tax returns for three to five years

6. Credit
___ Credit history of the business
___ Amount of credit available from suppliers and vendors
___ Terms of credit available from suppliers and other vendors

CONTROL CHECKLIST

1. Ownership Structure
___ Form of ownership*
___ Articles of incorporation; partnership and/or shareholder agreement
___ Name of principals with more than 25 percent ownership*
___ Name of minority shareholders
___ List of shareholders not employed by the business
___ Organization chart
___ Fictitious name registrations

2. Strategic Alliances
___ Vendor relationships
___ Franchise agreements*
___ Marketing and advertising agencies
___ Accounting firms
___ Law firms
___ Commitments of time and money vs. services rendered from above
___ Company attorney
___ Insurance agent

3. Employee Relationships
___ Employment contracts
___ Independent contractors and agreements
___ Employee manual
___ Job descriptions
___ Estimate of employee turnover rate and cost (ETOR and ETOC)*
___ Procedure to locate, assess and hire employees
___ Enforceable covenants not to compete
___ Employee training programs

4. Location
____ Property survey
____ Zoning classification and restrictions
____Easements on the property
____ Real estate taxes
____ Property appraisal*
____ Buildings and improvements*
____ Floor plan of buildings and location of improvements

5. Administrative
____ Licenses
____ Insurance plans and policies
____ Pending litigation*
____ Contingent liabilities*
____ Internet or Intranet-enabled administration procedures and protocols

MARKETING CHECKLIST

1. Business Mission Statement

2. Marketing Position

3. Marketing & Communication Strategy
____ Advertising and marketing themes and appeals*
____ Venues for spreading the marketing message
____ Advertising contracts
____ Agreements with advertising or marketing firms or agents
____ Samples of marketing and advertising materials
____ Marketing research to support position and strategy*

4. E-commerce Applications
____ Website address*
____ Number of hits per day
____ Conversion rate of hits to sales*
____ Links to other website providers
____ Description of business-to-business activity

5. Competitive Marketing Analysis
____ Description of nearest competitor
____ Number of competitors in trade area
____ Market share*
____ Marketing opportunities to expand current sales results

6. Growth Wall Analysis*
___ Negative trend of sales and profits
___ Obsolescence of product or service line
___ Unproductive advertising & marketing
___ Declining employee morale
___ No enhancements to product or services

A growth wall is a common condition that prevents progress and results. It stops a business dead in its tracks. The most obvious symptom is the end of a strong favorable trend of trailing revenue. It occurs because the environment around a business has changed but the business has not. For example, selling 8-track tape players was big business in the 1960s. Companies still attempting to sell them today would likely fail. The market has changed. Thus, a growth wall presents considerable increase in business risk.

It is important to recognize growth walls in business valuation, because a declining trend of business results often prompts an owner to consider selling his business. Value is falling. An entrepreneur, recognizing this phenomenon, is better armed to make adjustments that could return the business to an upward performance trend.

Professor Richard Osborne, Case Western Reserve University, describes the phase two (after the start-up has already passed) growth wall as common in the evolution of owner-managed entrepreneurial companies. He notes several patterns inherent in companies that fail to penetrate a growth wall, including 1) sudden reversals in revenue after steady annual business increases; 2) diminished entrepreneurial energy; 3) generalized internal focus; 4) falling behind the industry trend change curve; 5) reactive product or service development, distribution, and marketing; and 6) absence of internal attitudes and competencies necessary to see and understand external threats.

To break through a growth wall, company managers must reestablish the link between their product and their market—the latter has changed and the former has not. Business managers should study the environment in which the business operates to identify and recommend complimentary changes. The entrepreneur who can recognize a growth wall in a business, and has the ability to scale it, may enjoy highly lucrative business investment opportunities.

SALES CHECKLIST

1. Sales Results*
___ Sales data*
___ Annual trends
___ Seasonal trends
___ Time to create one sale
___ Average sales price
___ Average gross profit per sale

___ Average net profit per sale
___ Impact of sales cycles on cash flow*
___ Record of cash flows by month*
___ Record of deficit spending to sustain low sales months

2. Description of Product or Service
___ Transactional products
___ Consulting services
___ Enterprise relationships
___ Key benefit to customer*

3. Sales Channels
___ How sales leads are generated*
___ How sales are made*
___ Sales persons
___ Telemarketing
___ Direct mail
___ Internet
___ Other

4. Sales Management
___ Sales lines of authority
___ Sales person or employee span of control*
___ Number of accounts one can handle
___ Amount of sales floor one can handle
___ Sales compensation formula*
___ Base compensation
___ Commission income
___ Territorial assignments
___ Geographically-based
___ Product-based
___ Treatment of reimbursable expenses
___ Description of sales training

PRODUCTION CHECKLIST

1. Production
___ Capacity to produce under existing conditions
___ Limitations on capacity
___ Variance between existing capacity and demand*
___ Cost to increase capacity

2. List of Property
___ Equipment
___ Furnishings
___ Fixtures
___ Description of each of above
___ Age and condition of equipment
___ Obsolescence noted*
___ Deferred maintenance noted*

3. Inventory
___ Amount on hand to meet existing demand*
___ End of year (EOY) changes in quantity of inventory on hand
___ Inventory turnover ratio*
___ Annual cost of goods/inventory at cost
___ Accounting systems to identify inventory on hand and needed
___ Variance of inventory in peak versus low selling seasons
___ Source of inventory and timing of delivery

4. Schematic of Work Flow
___ Receipt of inventory
___ Storage of inventory
___ Description of production process if any*

SERVICE CHECKLIST

1. Services
___ Services performed*
___ Pricing structure for services
___ Turnaround time for service work
___ Who performs services to clients

2. Policies
___ Product or service guarantees
___ Returns & refunds*
___ Payment
___ Tracking system
___ Managing complaints
___ Annual cost of returns

3. Distribution of Service
___ Where service is performed
___ Profitability of service
___ How products are returned
___ Who pays cost of shipping

4. Training*
___ Staff training of new personnel
___ Employee education and seminars
___ Outsourced service department

5. Intellectual Capital
___ Unique sources*
___ Key people
___ Patents & copyrights
___ Production processes
___ Competitive intelligence
___ Customer relationships*
___ Institutionalized or related to key people
___ Transferability of intellectual capital
___ Control over intellectual capital
___ Vested rights
___ Non-disclosure agreements with key personnel

Index

B

C

Reminders, Opportunities and Ideas

Reminders, Opportunities and Ideas

Reminders, Opportunities and Ideas

Reminders, Opportunities and Ideas

Reminders, Opportunities and Ideas

Reminders, Opportunities and Ideas